4/10/21
cover damage
sn

◁ S0-ARK-474

C OCEAN

EUROPE
pages 32–37

A S I A
pages 38–43

PACIFIC

OCEAN

FRICA
ages 44–49

EQUATOR

INDIAN

OCEAN

AUSTRALIA
pages 50–55

A N T A R C T I C A
pages 56–59

NATIONAL GEOGRAPHIC
KiDS

BEGINNER'S WORLD ATLAS

NATIONAL GEOGRAPHIC
WASHINGTON, D.C.

Contents

Understanding Your World

This atlas uses maps and photographs to reveal the wonderful diversity of people, cultures, and the natural world that makes each place on Earth unique. Look for examples of diversity in the land and the people, ranging from traditional to modern lifestyles and from animals in the wild to bustling cities.

Making the Round Earth Flat

From your backyard Earth probably looks flat. If you could travel into space like an astronaut, you would see that Earth is a giant ball with blue oceans, greenish brown land, and white clouds. Even in space you can see only the part of Earth facing you. To see the whole Earth at one time, you need a map. Maps take the round Earth and make it flat, so you can see all of it at one time.

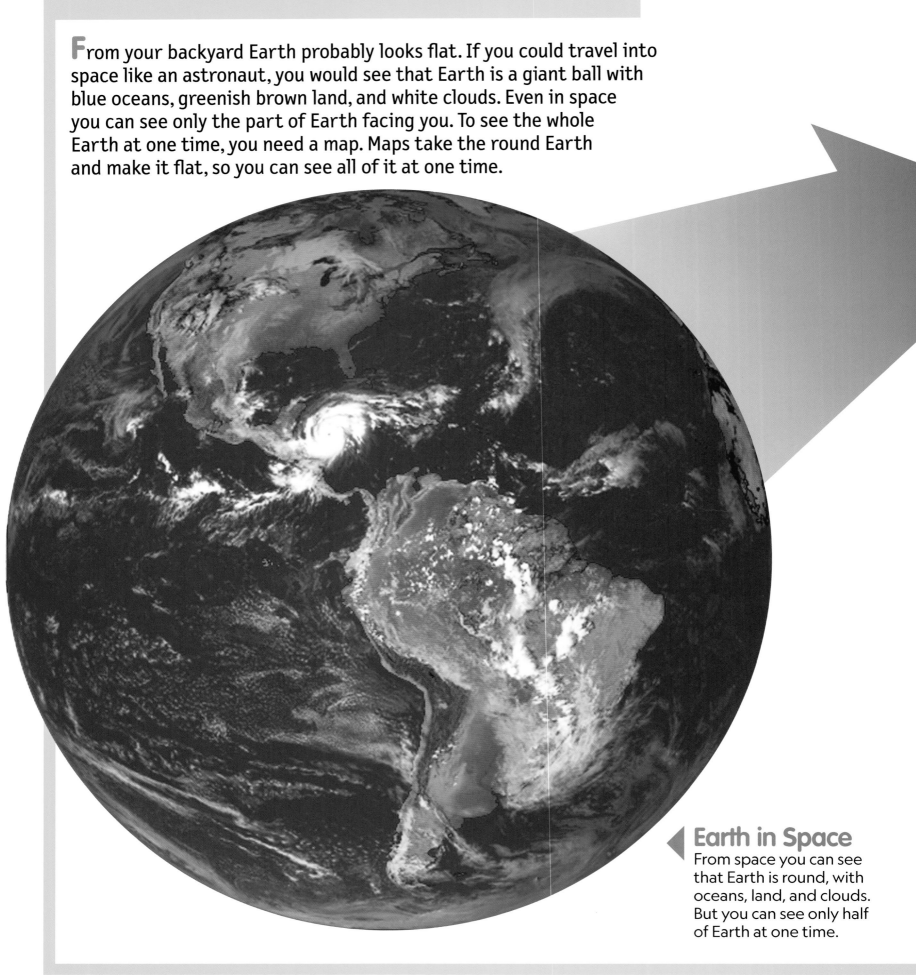

Earth in Space
From space you can see that Earth is round, with oceans, land, and clouds. But you can see only half of Earth at one time.

Earth as a Globe
A globe is a tiny model of Earth that you can put on a stand or hold in your hand. You still can't see all of Earth at one time. You have to turn the globe to see the other side.

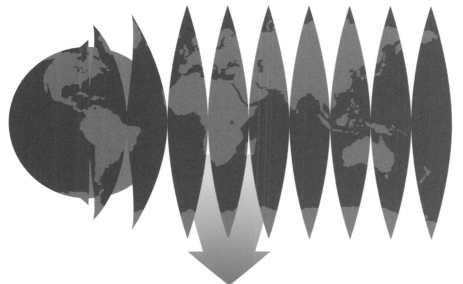

Earth on Paper
If you could peel a globe like an orange, you could make Earth flat, but there would be spaces between the pieces. Mapmakers stretch the land and the water at the top and bottom to fill in the spaces. This is how a map lets you see the whole world all at once.

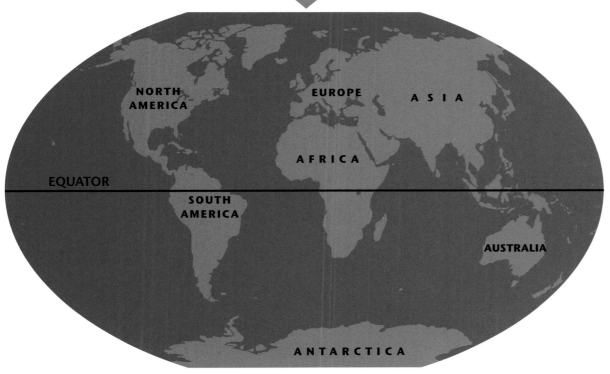

NORTH AMERICA

EUROPE

ASIA

AFRICA

EQUATOR

SOUTH AMERICA

AUSTRALIA

ANTARCTICA

The Equator
The Equator is an imaginary line around Earth's middle. It divides the world into two halves—the Northern Hemisphere and the Southern Hemisphere.

What Is a Map?

A map is a drawing of a place as it looks from above. It is flat, and it is smaller than the place it shows. A map can help you find where you are and where you want to go.

Mapping your backyard ...

... from the ground

From your backyard you see everything in front of you straight on. You have to look up to see your roof and the tops of trees. You can't see what's in front of your house.

... from higher up

From higher up you look down on things. You can see the tops of trees and things in your yard and into the yards of other houses in your neighborhood.

Finding Places on the Map

A map can help you get where you want to go. A map tells you how to read it by showing you a compass rose, a scale, and a key.

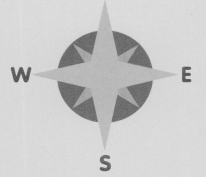

A compass rose helps you travel in the right direction. It tells you where north (N), south (S), east (E), and west (W) are on your map.

Some maps have only a north arrow.

| 0 | 300 | 600 miles |
| 0 | 450 | 900 kilometers |

In the scale above, the upper bar represents distance in miles. The lower bar represents distance in kilometers.

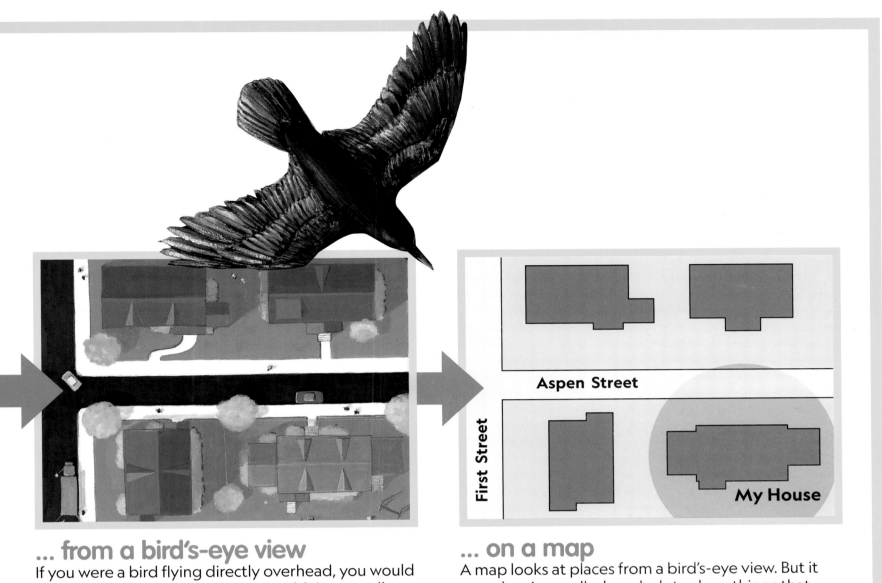

... from a bird's-eye view

If you were a bird flying directly overhead, you would see only the tops of things. You wouldn't see walls, tree trunks, tires, or feet.

... on a map

A map looks at places from a bird's-eye view. But it uses drawings called symbols to show things that don't move, such as these houses.

A map key helps you understand symbols used on the map to show things like mountains, deserts, grasslands, or boundaries.

Map Key

- Mountain
- Desert
- Coniferous forest
- Deciduous forest
- Rain forest
- Grassland
- Wetland
- Tundra
- Volcano
- Dry salt lake
- Europe-Asia boundary

What This Atlas Will Teach You

You hold the world in your hands as you turn the pages of this atlas. Physical maps will show you natural features, and political maps will show you countries and other places created by people.

Desert, North America

Coral reef, Pacific Ocean

THE PHYSICAL WORLD

 Land regions You will find out what kinds of land cover a continent. Does it have mountains and deserts? If so, where are they?

 Water You will learn about a continent's chief lakes, rivers, and waterfalls. You'll see that some continents have more water than others.

 Climate Climate is the weather of a place over many years. Some continents are colder and wetter or hotter and drier than others.

 Plants You'll discover what kinds of plants grow on a particular continent.

 Animals Continents each have certain kinds of animals. Did you know that tigers live in the wild only in Asia?

Mountains, Asia

Sugarcane farmer, Malawi

ARCTIC OCEAN

Greenland
(Denmark)

NORWAY

ICELAND

FINLAND   R U S S I A

CANADA

UNITED
KINGDOM

UKRAINE KAZAKHSTAN MONGOLIA

FRANCE

UNITED
STATES

SPAIN   TURKEY   JAPAN
SYRIA   IRAN

MOROCCO   C H I N A   PACIFIC

MEXICO   ALGERIA LIBYA EGYPT   OCEAN
SAUDI   INDIA
CUBA   ARABIA   VIETNAM

MAURITANIA   THAILAND   PHILIPPINES

NICARAGUA   VENEZUELA   MALI NIGER CHAD
GUYANA   SUDAN
COLOMBIA   SURINAME   ETHIOPIA

PACIFIC   LIBERIA   SOMALIA

ECUADOR   DEMOCRATIC
OCEAN   NIGERIA   REPUBLIC   EQUATOR   INDONESIA   PAPUA
OF THE   NEW GUINEA
PERU   BRAZIL   CONGO TANZANIA

BOLIVIA   ANGOLA
ZAMBIA

PARAGUAY   NAMIBIA   MADAGASCAR

CHILE   URUGUAY   SOUTH   INDIAN   AUSTRALIA
AFRICA
ARGENTINA   OCEAN
NEW
ZEALAND

A N T A R C T I C A

THE POLITICAL WORLD

Countries You will learn about the countries that make up a continent. Maps in this atlas show country names in type like this: **UNITED STATES.**

Cities You will find out which cities are the most populous on a continent. The map key will tell you which cities are capitals.

People You will learn where groups of people on a continent come from, where they live, what they do, how they have fun, and more.

Languages Many languages are spoken on most continents. Here you will find out which languages most people speak.

Vancouver, Canada

Schoolgirls, Vietnam

The Physical World

A physical map uses symbols to show where mountains, deserts, forests, and other features of the land are.

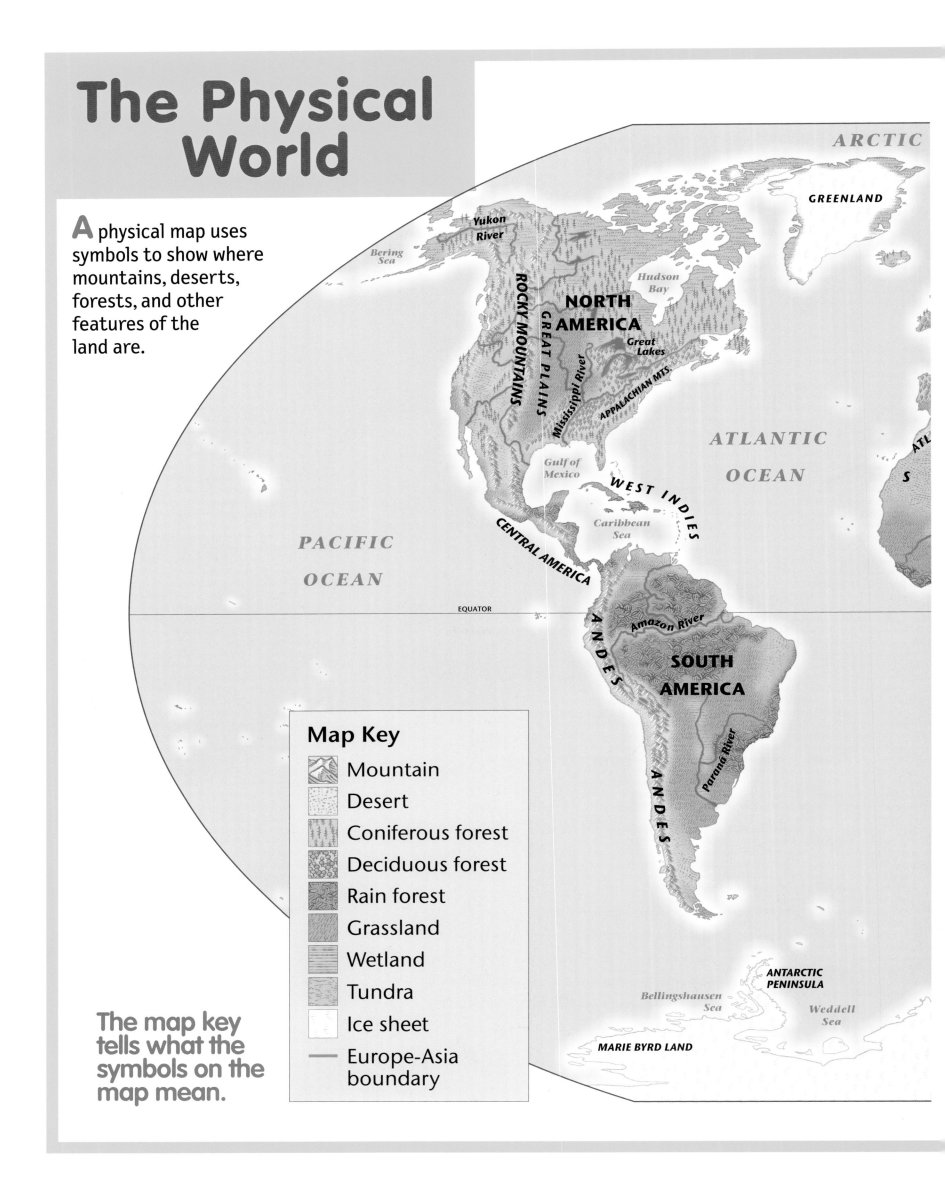

ARCTIC

GREENLAND

Yukon River

Bering Sea

Hudson Bay

ROCKY MOUNTAINS

GREAT PLAINS

NORTH AMERICA

Great Lakes

Mississippi River

APPALACHIAN MTS.

Gulf of Mexico

WEST INDIES

ATLANTIC OCEAN

ATL S

PACIFIC OCEAN

Caribbean Sea

CENTRAL AMERICA

EQUATOR

ANDES

Amazon River

SOUTH AMERICA

Paraná River

ANDES

ANTARCTIC PENINSULA

Bellingshausen Sea

Weddell Sea

MARIE BYRD LAND

Map Key

- Mountain
- Desert
- Coniferous forest
- Deciduous forest
- Rain forest
- Grassland
- Wetland
- Tundra
- Ice sheet
- — Europe-Asia boundary

The map key tells what the symbols on the map mean.

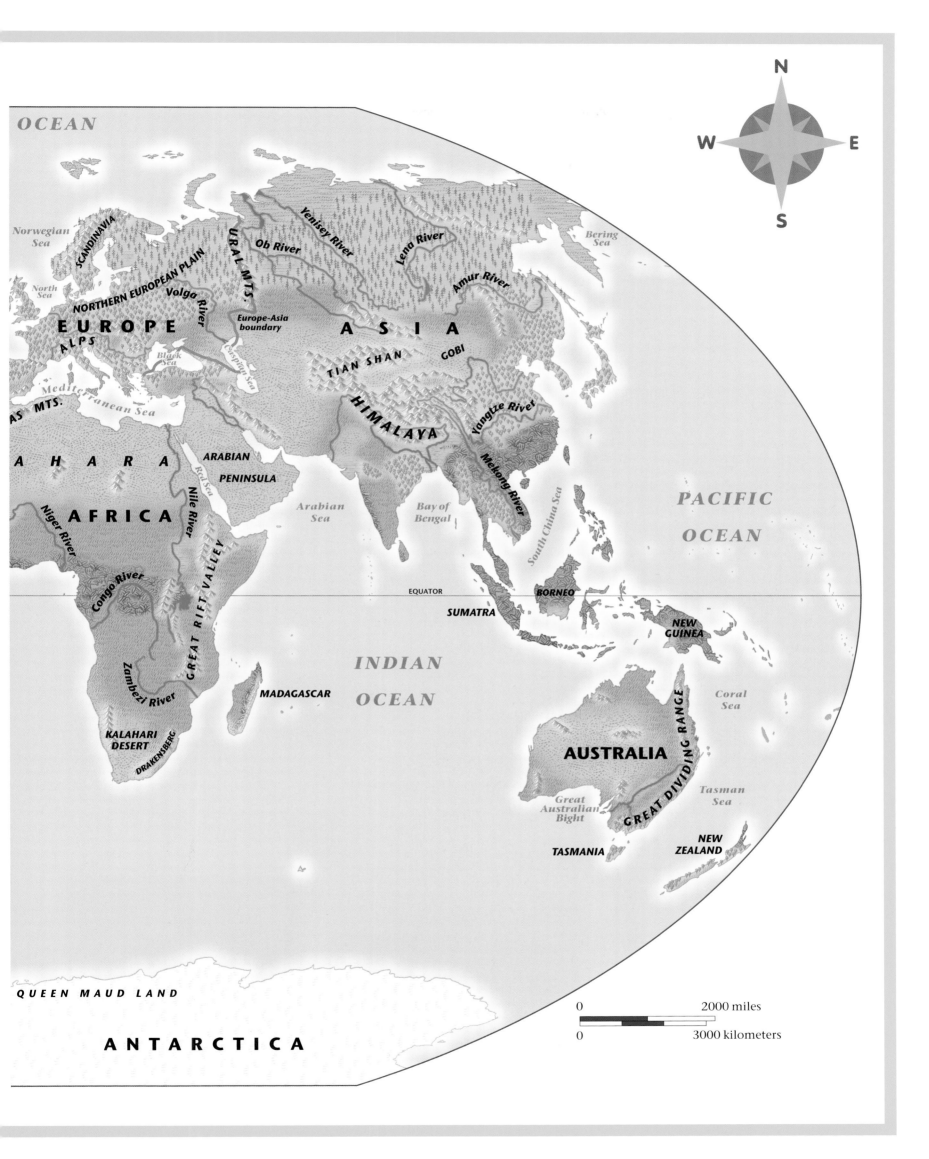

N
W   E
S

OCEAN

Norwegian Sea

SCANDINAVIA

North Sea

NORTHERN EUROPEAN PLAIN

U R A L   M T S.

Volga River

Ob River

Yenisey River

Lena River

Amur River

Bering Sea

EUROPE

ALPS

Europe-Asia boundary

A S I A

Black Sea

Caspian Sea

TIAN SHAN

GOBI

Mediterranean Sea

AS   MTS.

H I M A L A Y A

Yangtze River

S A H A R A

ARABIAN PENINSULA

Red Sea

AFRICA

Arabian Sea

Bay of Bengal

Mekong River

Niger River

Nile River

PACIFIC

OCEAN

Congo River

GREAT RIFT VALLEY

South China Sea

EQUATOR

BORNEO

SUMATRA

NEW GUINEA

Zambezi River

INDIAN

OCEAN

MADAGASCAR

Coral Sea

KALAHARI DESERT

DRAKENSBERG

GREAT DIVIDING RANGE

AUSTRALIA

Tasman Sea

Great Australian Bight

NEW ZEALAND

TASMANIA

QUEEN MAUD LAND

0   2000 miles

0   3000 kilometers

A N T A R C T I C A

The Physical World Close Up

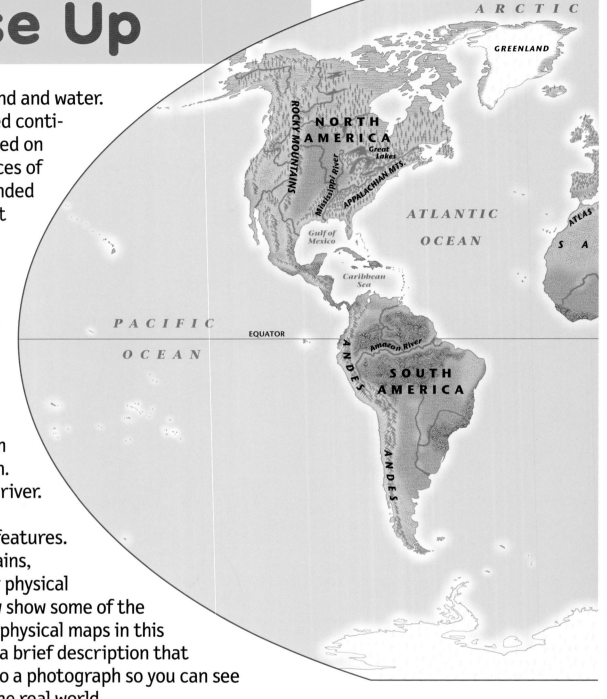

Earth's surface is made up of land and water. The biggest landmasses are called continents. All seven of them are named on this map. Islands are smaller pieces of land that are completely surrounded by water. Greenland is the largest island. A peninsula is land that is almost entirely surrounded by water. Europe has lots of them.

Oceans are the largest bodies of water on Earth. Can you find all four oceans? Lakes are bodies of water surrounded by land, like the Great Lakes, in North America. A river is a large stream that flows into a lake or an ocean. The Nile, in Africa, is the longest river.

These are Earth's main physical features. But continents also have mountains, deserts, forests, and many other physical features. The map symbols below show some of the features that will appear on the physical maps in this atlas. Each symbol is followed by a brief description that explains its meaning. There is also a photograph so you can see what each feature looks like in the real world.

 Mountain
Land rising at least 1,000 feet (305 m) above Earth's surface

Desert
Very dry land that can be hot or cold and sandy or rocky

 Coniferous forest
Forest with trees that have seed cones and often needlelike leaves

O C E A N

EUROPE

ASIA

URAL MTS.

Volga
River

Europe-Asia
boundary

Gobi

ALPS

HIMALAYA

Yangtze River

Mediterranean Sea

MTS.

HARA

PACIFIC

OCEAN

AFRICA

Nile River

EQUATOR

INDIAN

OCEAN

AUSTRALIA

GREAT DIVIDING RANGE

ANTARCTICA

0   2000 miles

0   3000 kilometers

 Ice sheet
A permanent layer of thick ice that covers the land, as in Antarctica

 Tundra
A cold region with low plants that grow only during warm months

 Wetland
Land, such as a marsh or swamp, that is mostly covered with water

 Deciduous forest
Forest with trees that change colors and lose leaves in the fall

 Rain forest
Forest that needs lots of water and has trees up to 200 feet (61 m) tall

 Grassland
A grass-covered area with too little rain for many trees to grow

The Political World

Political maps show places where people live. This one names countries and territories of the world.

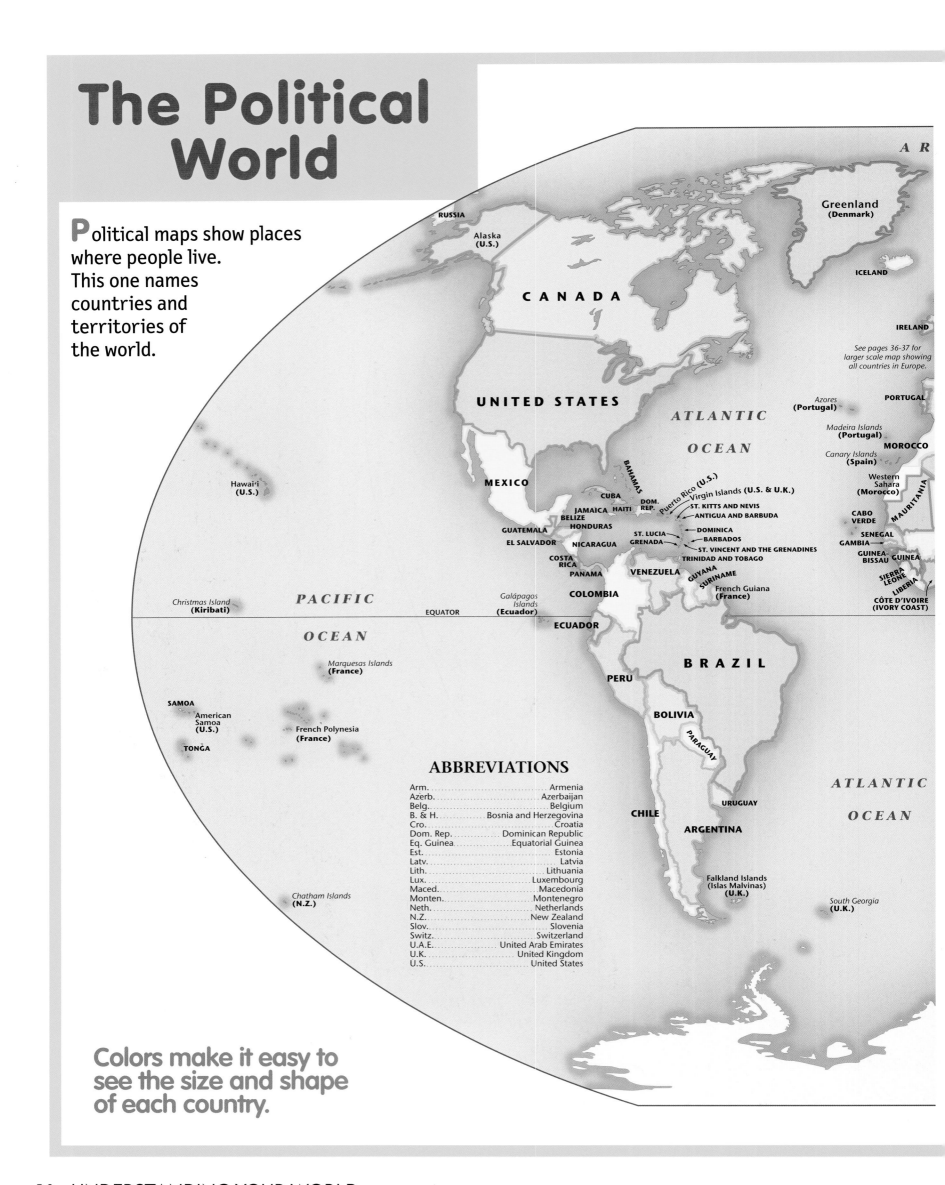

RUSSIA

Alaska
(U.S.)

CANADA

UNITED STATES

Hawai'i
(U.S.)

MEXICO

ATLANTIC

OCEAN

BAHAMAS

CUBA
JAMAICA HAITI
BELIZE
HONDURAS
GUATEMALA
EL SALVADOR NICARAGUA
COSTA
RICA
PANAMA

DOM.
REP. Puerto Rico (U.S.)
Virgin Islands (U.S. & U.K.)
ST. KITTS AND NEVIS
ANTIGUA AND BARBUDA
DOMINICA
ST. LUCIA BARBADOS
GRENADA
ST. VINCENT AND THE GRENADINES
TRINIDAD AND TOBAGO

VENEZUELA GUYANA
SURINAME
French Guiana
(France)

COLOMBIA

Galápagos
Islands
(Ecuador)

EQUATOR

ECUADOR

BRAZIL

PERU

BOLIVIA

PARAGUAY

CHILE

URUGUAY

ARGENTINA

Falkland Islands
(Islas Malvinas)
(U.K.)

South Georgia
(U.K.)

Greenland
(Denmark)

ICELAND

IRELAND

See pages 36-37 for
larger scale map showing
all countries in Europe.

PORTUGAL

Azores
(Portugal)

Madeira Islands
(Portugal) MOROCCO

Canary Islands
(Spain)

Western
Sahara
(Morocco)

MAURITANIA

CABO
VERDE

SENEGAL
GAMBIA
GUINEA- GUINEA
BISSAU
SIERRA
LEONE
LIBERIA
CÔTE D'IVOIRE
(IVORY COAST)

A R

PACIFIC

OCEAN

Christmas Island
(Kiribati)

Marquesas Islands
(France)

SAMOA
American
Samoa
(U.S.)
TONGA

French Polynesia
(France)

Chatham Islands
(N.Z.)

ATLANTIC

OCEAN

ABBREVIATIONS

Arm.	Armenia
Azerb.	Azerbaijan
Belg.	Belgium
B. & H.	Bosnia and Herzegovina
Cro.	Croatia
Dom. Rep.	Dominican Republic
Eq. Guinea	Equatorial Guinea
Est.	Estonia
Latv.	Latvia
Lith.	Lithuania
Lux.	Luxembourg
Maced.	Macedonia
Monten.	Montenegro
Neth.	Netherlands
N.Z.	New Zealand
Slov.	Slovenia
Switz.	Switzerland
U.A.E.	United Arab Emirates
U.K.	United Kingdom
U.S.	United States

Colors make it easy to
see the size and shape
of each country.

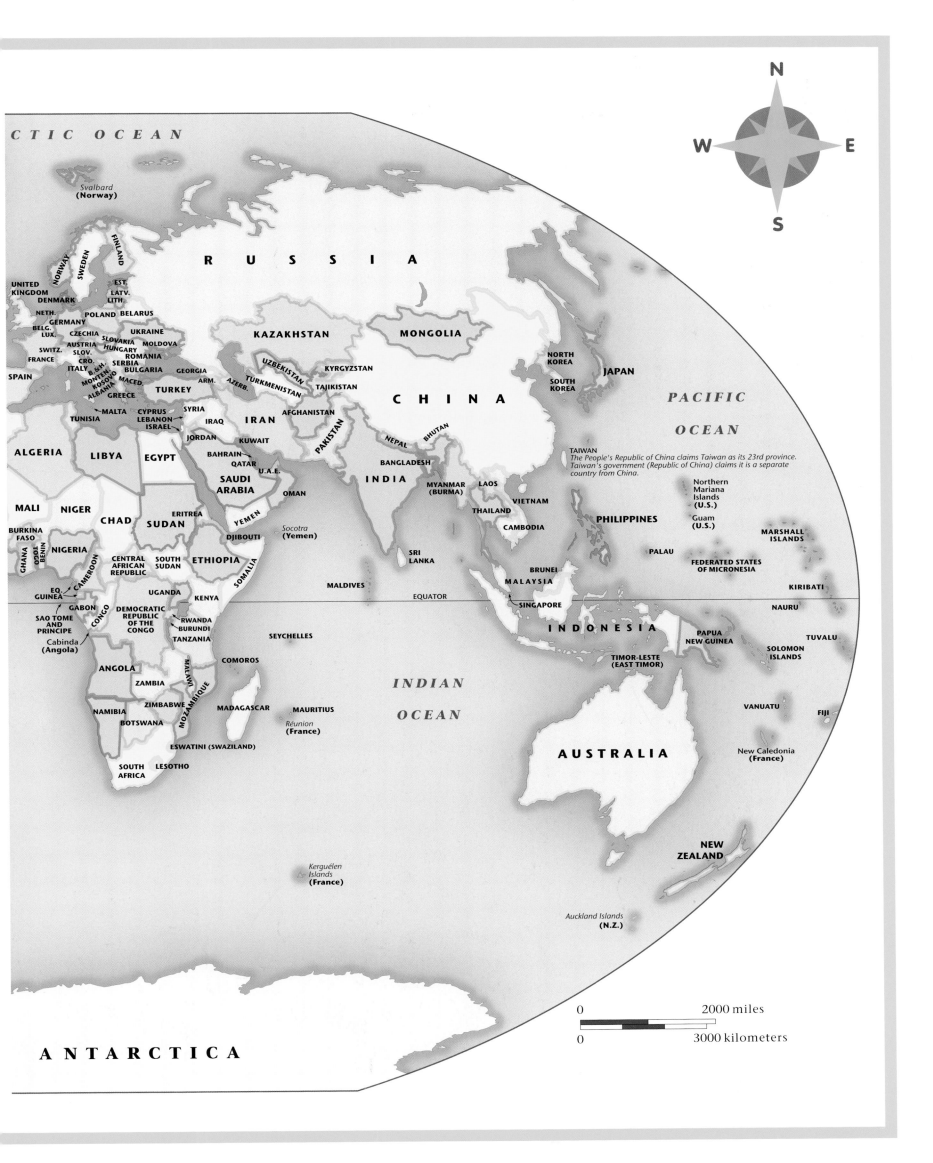

CTIC OCEAN

Svalbard
(Norway)

NORWAY
SWEDEN
FINLAND
UNITED
KINGDOM
DENMARK
EST.
LATV.
LITH.
NETH.
BELG.
LUX.
GERMANY
POLAND
BELARUS
CZECHIA
SLOVAKIA
UKRAINE
AUSTRIA
HUNGARY
SWITZ.
SLOV.
ROMANIA
FRANCE
ITALY
CRO.
B.&H.
SERBIA
MOLDOVA
MONTEN.
KOSOVO
MACED.
BULGARIA
ALBANIA
GREECE
GEORGIA
ARM.
AZERB.
SPAIN
TURKEY

R U S S I A

KAZAKHSTAN

MONGOLIA

NORTH
KOREA

JAPAN

SOUTH
KOREA

C H I N A

PACIFIC

OCEAN

UZBEKISTAN
KYRGYZSTAN
TURKMENISTAN
TAJIKISTAN

MALTA
TUNISIA
CYPRUS
LEBANON
ISRAEL
SYRIA
IRAQ
IRAN
AFGHANISTAN
JORDAN
KUWAIT
PAKISTAN
NEPAL
BHUTAN

ALGERIA
LIBYA
EGYPT
BAHRAIN
QATAR
U.A.E.
SAUDI
ARABIA
OMAN
BANGLADESH
INDIA
MYANMAR
(BURMA)
LAOS

TAIWAN
The People's Republic of China claims Taiwan as its 23rd province.
Taiwan's government (Republic of China) claims it is a separate
country from China.

Northern
Mariana
Islands
(U.S.)

MALI
NIGER
CHAD
SUDAN
ERITREA
YEMEN
DJIBOUTI
Socotra
(Yemen)
THAILAND
VIETNAM
CAMBODIA
PHILIPPINES
Guam
(U.S.)
MARSHALL
ISLANDS

BURKINA
FASO
NIGERIA
CENTRAL
AFRICAN
REPUBLIC
SOUTH
SUDAN
ETHIOPIA
SOMALIA
SRI
LANKA
PALAU
FEDERATED STATES
OF MICRONESIA

GHANA
TOGO
BENIN
CAMEROON
EQ.
GUINEA
GABON
SAO TOME
AND
PRINCIPE
Cabinda
(Angola)
CONGO
DEMOCRATIC
REPUBLIC
OF THE
CONGO
UGANDA
KENYA
RWANDA
BURUNDI
TANZANIA
SEYCHELLES
MALDIVES
EQUATOR
BRUNEI
MALAYSIA
SINGAPORE
KIRIBATI
NAURU

I N D O N E S I A
PAPUA
NEW GUINEA
TUVALU
SOLOMON
ISLANDS

ANGOLA
ZAMBIA
MALAWI
COMOROS
TIMOR-LESTE
(EAST TIMOR)

NAMIBIA
ZIMBABWE
BOTSWANA
MOZAMBIQUE
MADAGASCAR
MAURITIUS
Réunion
(France)
I N D I A N

OCEAN
VANUATU
FIJI

ESWATINI (SWAZILAND)
SOUTH
AFRICA
LESOTHO
A U S T R A L I A
New Caledonia
(France)

*Kerguélen
Islands*
(France)
NEW
ZEALAND

Auckland Islands
(N.Z.)

A N T A R C T I C A

N
W   E
S

0   2000 miles
0   3000 kilometers

NORTH AMERICA

North America is shaped like a triangle. It is wide in the north. In the south, it becomes a strip of land only 30 miles (48 km) wide at its narrowest point. There, the Panama Canal connects the Atlantic and Pacific Oceans. The warm islands in the Caribbean Sea are part of North America. So is icy Greenland in the far north. The seven countries between Mexico and South America make up a region commonly called Central America. It connects the rest of North America to South America.

A polar bear roams the icy shore of Hudson Bay in Manitoba, Canada, in search of food.

The Golden Gate Bridge stretches high above the entrance to San Francisco Bay in California, U.S.A.

NORTH AMERICA

 LAND REGIONS The Rocky Mountains stretch through western North America into Mexico, where the mountains are called the Sierra Madre Oriental. Older, lower mountains called the Appalachians are in the east. Grassy plains lie between these two mountain chains.

 WATER Together, the Mississippi and its tributary the Missouri make up the continent's longest river. The Great Lakes are the world's largest group of freshwater lakes.

 CLIMATE The far north is icy cold. Temperatures get warmer as you move south. Deserts cover dry areas in the southwest, but much of Central America is wet and hot.

 PLANTS Large forests grow where rain or snow is plentiful. Grasslands cover areas with less precipitation.

 ANIMALS There is a big variety of animals—everything from bears, moose, and wolves to monkeys and colorful parrots.

A white-tailed deer nuzzles her babies in a meadow near the Great Lakes. Deer live in almost every country on the continent.

North America is famous for its deciduous forests. Leaves turn fiery colors each fall.

Palm trees grow along sandy beaches on islands in the Caribbean Sea. In this part of North America the weather is warm year-round.

Dragonlike iguanas live in the rain forests of Mexico and Central America. This harmless lizard can grow as long as a man's leg.

Deserts are found in the southwestern part of North America. The large rock formation on the right is called The Mitten. Can you guess why?

NORTH AMERICA

Denali
(Mt. McKinley)
Highest point in
North America

N

ASIA

ARCTIC
OCEAN

Brooks Range

Yukon
River

GREENLAND

Mackenzie River

Great
Bear Lake

Great
Slave Lake

Hudson
Bay

This view from a
plane shows that
Greenland has
high mountains
and lots of snow
and ice.

COAST MOUNTAINS

R O C K Y   M O U N T A I N S

Cascade Range

Columbia River

Sierra Nevada

Colorado River

Death Valley
Lowest point in
North America

G R E A T   P L A I N S

Missouri River

Lake
Winnipeg

Mississippi
River

Great Lakes

APPALACHIAN MOUNTAINS

Ohio River

Mississippi
River

ATLANTIC
OCEAN

Map Key

Mountain

Desert

Coniferous forest

Deciduous forest

Rain forest

Grassland

Wetland

Tundra

Ice sheet

Volcano

■ Point of interest

PACIFIC
OCEAN

SIERRA MADRE OCCIDENTAL

SIERRA MADRE ORIENTAL

Rio Grande

Gulf of Mexico

W E S T

I N D I E S

Yucatan
Peninsula

CENTRAL AMERICA

Caribbean Sea

SOUTH AMERICA

0   600 miles

0   900 kilometers

NORTH AMERICA **19**

NORTH AMERICA

Snowboarding and skiing are popular sports in mountain areas.

This farmer is harvesting wheat on a big farm in Canada. Canada and the United States grow much of the world's wheat.

 COUNTRIES Canada, the United States, Mexico, and the countries of Central America and the West Indies make up North America.

 CITIES Mexico City is the most populous city in North America followed by the U.S. cities of New York and Los Angeles. Santo Domingo, in the Dominican Republic, is the most populous city in the West Indies.

 PEOPLE Ancestors of most people in North America came from Europe. Many other people trace their roots to Africa and Asia. Various groups of Native Americans live throughout the continent.

 LANGUAGES English and Spanish are the main languages. A large number of people in Canada and Haiti speak French. There are also many Native American languages.

The Angel of Independence monument in Mexico City commemorates Mexico's independence from Spain in 1821.

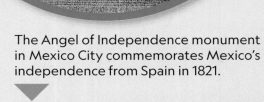

These red berries hold coffee beans. Many farmers in Guatemala make a living growing coffee.

These children from the country of Trinidad and Tobago in the West Indies are dressed up to celebrate a festival called Carnival.

Cliff Palace, part of Mesa Verde National Park, in Colorado, U.S.A., was built long ago by Native Americans. It is the largest cliff dwelling in North America.

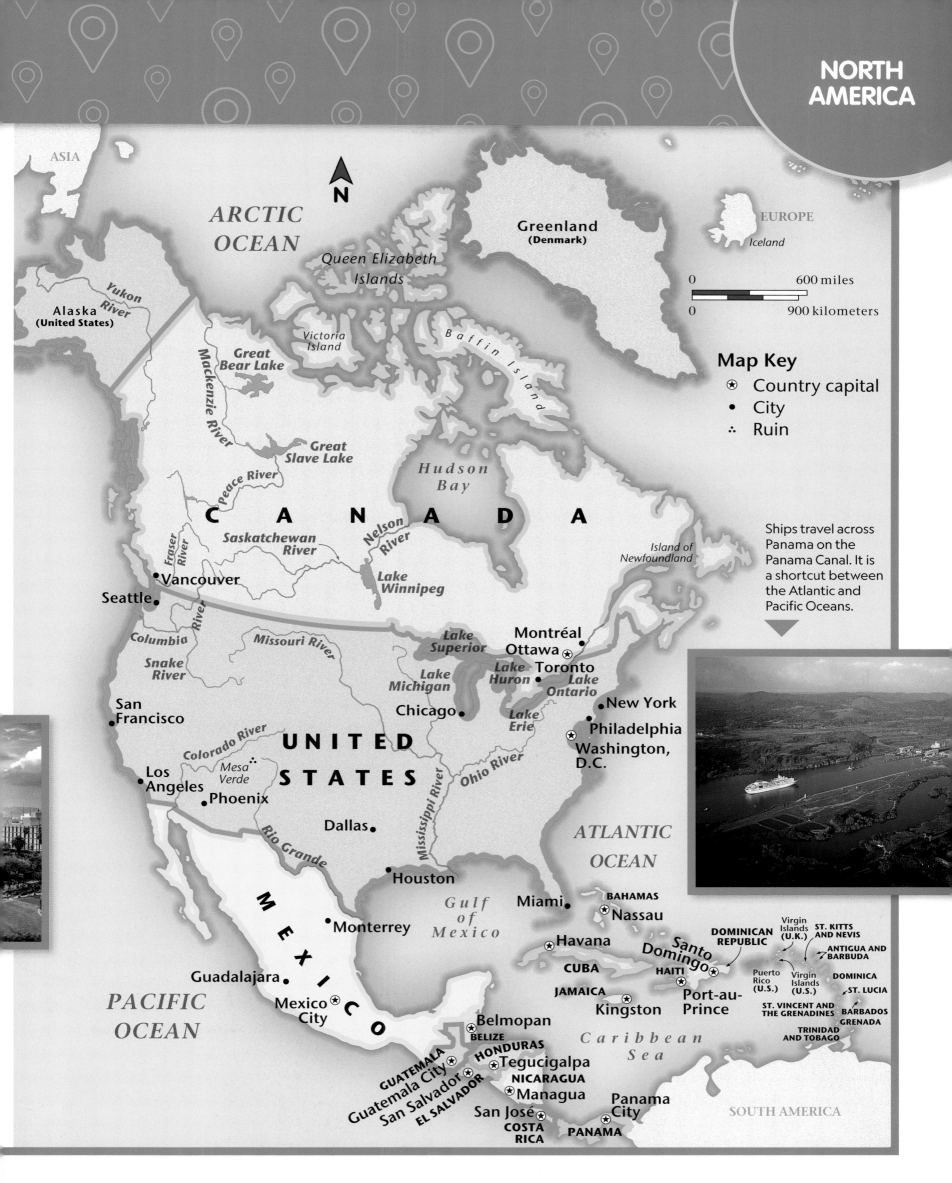

ASIA

ARCTIC
OCEAN

Greenland
(Denmark)

EUROPE

Iceland

Yukon
River

Alaska
(United States)

Queen Elizabeth
Islands

Victoria
Island

Baffin Island

0   600 miles

0   900 kilometers

Map Key
- ⊛ Country capital
- • City
- ∴ Ruin

Great
Bear Lake

Mackenzie River

Great
Slave Lake

Peace River

Hudson
Bay

C A N A D A

Island of
Newfoundland

Ships travel across
Panama on the
Panama Canal. It is
a shortcut between
the Atlantic and
Pacific Oceans.

Fraser
River

Saskatchewan
River

Nelson
River

Lake
Winnipeg

Vancouver

Seattle

River

Columbia

Missouri River

Lake
Superior

Montréal
Ottawa ⊛

Snake
River

Lake
Michigan

Lake
Huron

Toronto

Lake
Ontario

San
Francisco

U N I T E D
S T A T E S

Chicago

Lake
Erie

New York

Philadelphia
⊛ Washington,
D.C.

Los
Angeles

Colorado River

Mesa
Verde

Phoenix

Mississippi River

Ohio River

ATLANTIC
OCEAN

Dallas

Rio Grande

M E X I C O

Houston

Gulf
of
Mexico

Miami

BAHAMAS

Nassau

Virgin
Islands
(U.K.)

ST. KITTS
AND NEVIS

Monterrey

Havana

DOMINICAN
REPUBLIC

ANTIGUA AND
BARBUDA

Guadalajara

CUBA

Santo
Domingo

HAITI

Puerto
Rico
(U.S.)

Virgin
Islands
(U.S.)

DOMINICA

PACIFIC
OCEAN

Mexico
City ⊛

JAMAICA

Kingston

Port-au-
Prince

ST. LUCIA

ST. VINCENT AND
THE GRENADINES

BARBADOS

GRENADA

⊛ Belmopan

BELIZE

Caribbean
Sea

TRINIDAD
AND TOBAGO

GUATEMALA

Guatemala City ⊛

HONDURAS

⊛ Tegucigalpa

San Salvador ⊛

NICARAGUA

EL SALVADOR

⊛ Managua

Panama
City

SOUTH AMERICA

San José ⊛

COSTA
RICA

PANAMA

UNITED STATES

STATES The United States is made up of 50 states. Alaska and Hawai'i are separated from the rest of the country. So you can see them close up, they are shown near the bottom of the map. Use the small globe above to see their real locations.

CITIES Washington, D.C., is the national capital. Each state also has a capital city. New York City has the most people.

PEOPLE People from almost every country in the world live in the United States. Most live and work in and around cities.

LANGUAGES English is the chief language, followed by Spanish.

Chinese New Year is a big celebration in San Francisco, California. Lots of Chinese Americans live there.

Softball is a popular sport in the United States along with baseball, soccer, basketball, and football. This girl is getting ready to swing her bat in a softball game.

A scarecrow stands guard over a field of sunflowers in Kansas.

Sandy beaches, like this one in Delaware, are popular places to visit in the summer.

Seattle
Olympia
WASHINGTON
Portland
Salem
OREGON
Boise
ID
Columbia River

C
A
L
I
F
O
R
N
I
A
Carson City
Sacramento
San Francisco
San Jose
NEVADA
Las Vegas
Los Angeles
San Diego
AR

PACIFIC OCEAN

ALASKA
Juneau

0   400 miles
0   600 kilometers

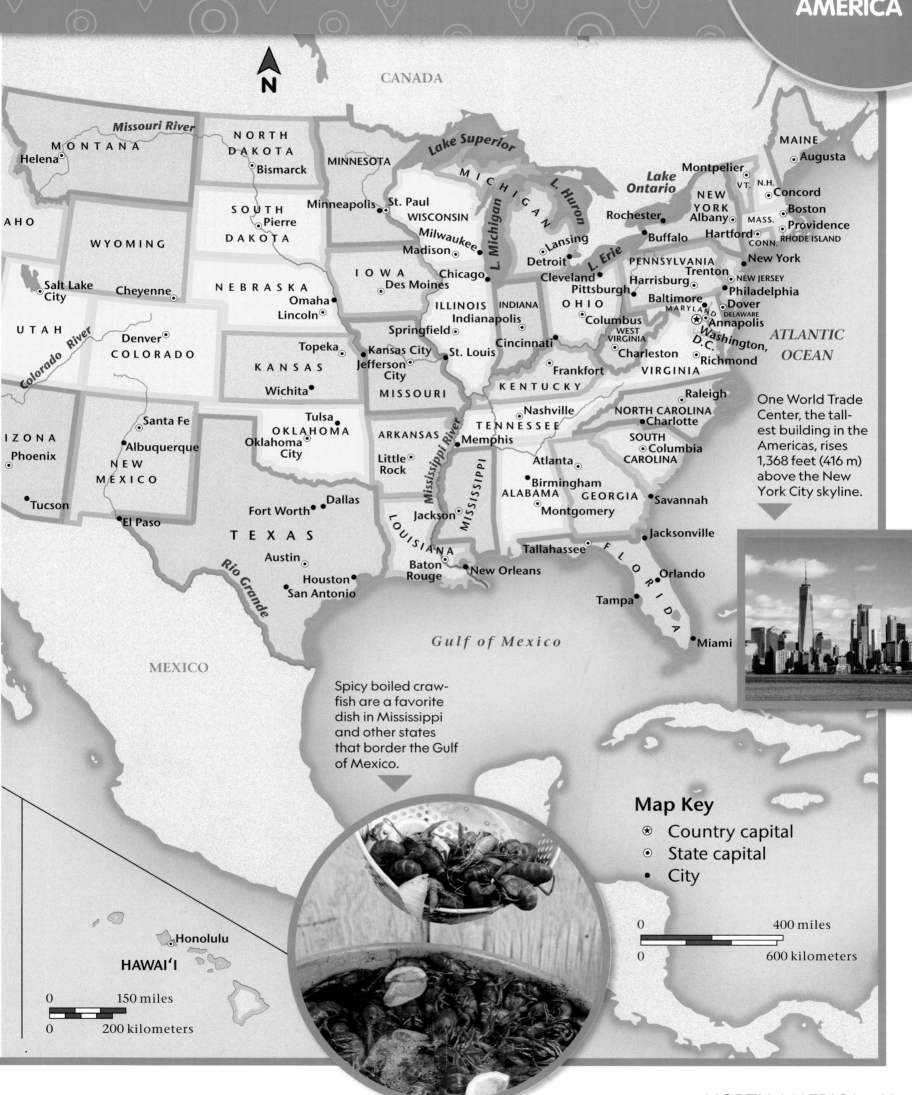

CANADA

N

Missouri River

MONTANA
Helena

NORTH DAKOTA
Bismarck

MINNESOTA

Lake Superior

MAINE
Augusta

Montpelier

VT. N.H.
Concord

SOUTH DAKOTA
Pierre

Minneapolis
St. Paul
WISCONSIN
Milwaukee
Madison

MICHIGAN
L. Michigan

L. Huron

Lake Ontario

NEW YORK
Albany

MASS.
Boston
Providence

Rochester

Buffalo

Hartford
CONN.
RHODE ISLAND

WYOMING

IDAHO

IOWA
Des Moines

Lansing

Detroit

L. Erie

PENNSYLVANIA

Trenton

New York

Salt Lake City
Cheyenne

NEBRASKA
Omaha
Lincoln

Chicago

ILLINOIS
Springfield

INDIANA
Indianapolis

Cleveland
Pittsburgh

OHIO
Columbus

Harrisburg

NEW JERSEY
Philadelphia
Baltimore
Dover
DELAWARE

UTAH

Denver
COLORADO

Topeka
Kansas City
Jefferson City

St. Louis

Cincinnati

MARYLAND

Annapolis
Washington, D.C.

ATLANTIC OCEAN

Colorado River

KANSAS

WEST VIRGINIA
Charleston

Richmond

Santa Fe

Wichita

MISSOURI

KENTUCKY
Frankfort

VIRGINIA

Raleigh

ARIZONA

Tulsa

OKLAHOMA
Oklahoma City

ARKANSAS

Mississippi River

TENNESSEE
Nashville

Memphis

NORTH CAROLINA
Charlotte

One World Trade Center, the tallest building in the Americas, rises 1,368 feet (416 m) above the New York City skyline.

Albuquerque

NEW MEXICO

Phoenix

Little Rock

SOUTH CAROLINA
Columbia

Tucson

El Paso

Fort Worth
Dallas

Jackson

MISSISSIPPI

Atlanta

Birmingham
ALABAMA

GEORGIA
Montgomery

Savannah

TEXAS
Austin

LOUISIANA

Baton Rouge
New Orleans

Tallahassee

FLORIDA

Jacksonville

Orlando

Houston
San Antonio

Rio Grande

Tampa

Miami

Gulf of Mexico

MEXICO

Spicy boiled crawfish are a favorite dish in Mississippi and other states that border the Gulf of Mexico.

Map Key
- ⊛ Country capital
- ◉ State capital
- • City

Honolulu

HAWAI'I

0   150 miles
0   200 kilometers

0   400 miles
0   600 kilometers

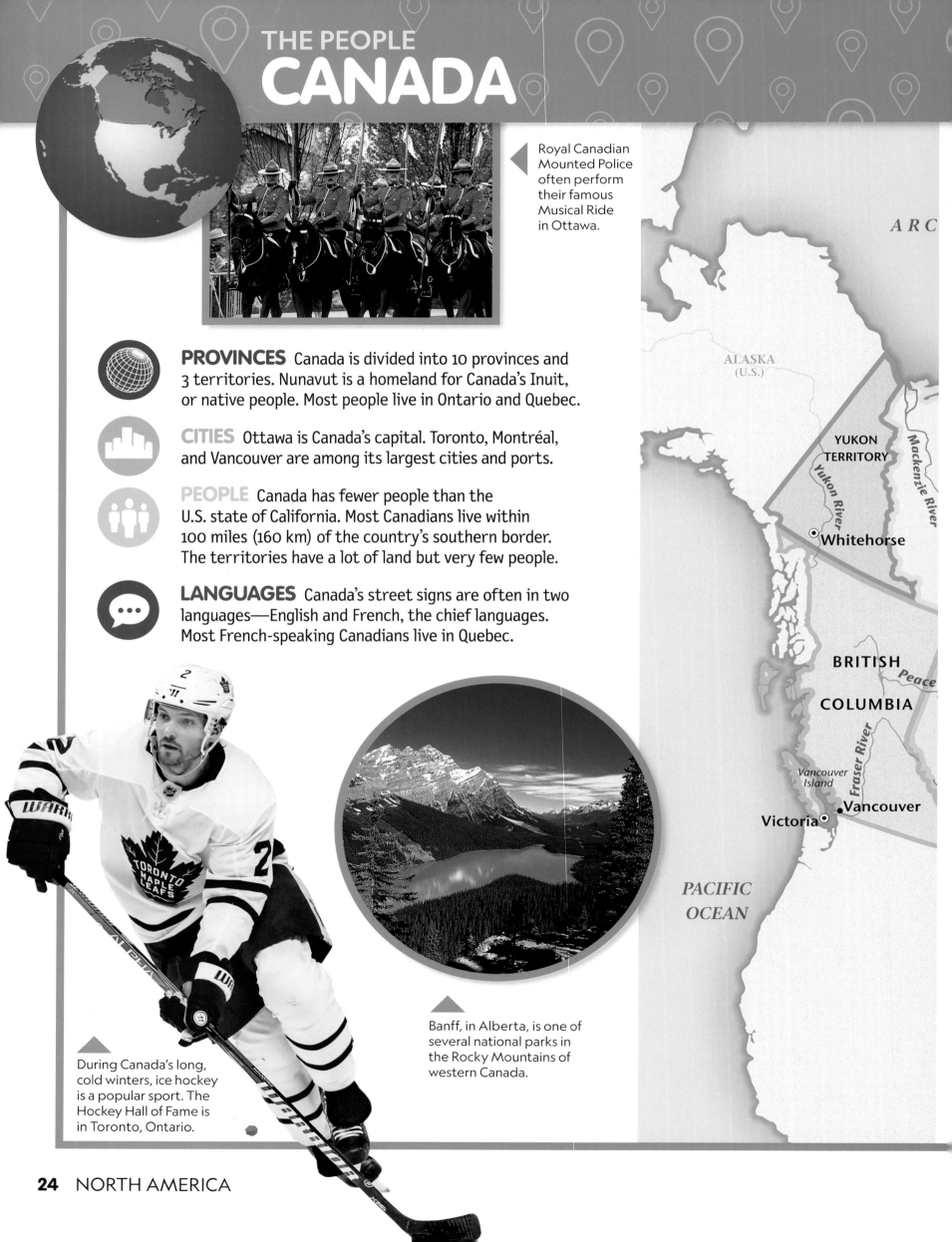

Royal Canadian Mounted Police often perform their famous Musical Ride in Ottawa.

PROVINCES Canada is divided into 10 provinces and 3 territories. Nunavut is a homeland for Canada's Inuit, or native people. Most people live in Ontario and Quebec.

CITIES Ottawa is Canada's capital. Toronto, Montréal, and Vancouver are among its largest cities and ports.

PEOPLE Canada has fewer people than the U.S. state of California. Most Canadians live within 100 miles (160 km) of the country's southern border. The territories have a lot of land but very few people.

LANGUAGES Canada's street signs are often in two languages—English and French, the chief languages. Most French-speaking Canadians live in Quebec.

During Canada's long, cold winters, ice hockey is a popular sport. The Hockey Hall of Fame is in Toronto, Ontario.

Banff, in Alberta, is one of several national parks in the Rocky Mountains of western Canada.

ARC

ALASKA (U.S.)

YUKON TERRITORY

Mackenzie River

Yukon River

⊙Whitehorse

BRITISH

Peace

COLUMBIA

Fraser River

Vancouver Island

Victoria⊙ •Vancouver

PACIFIC OCEAN

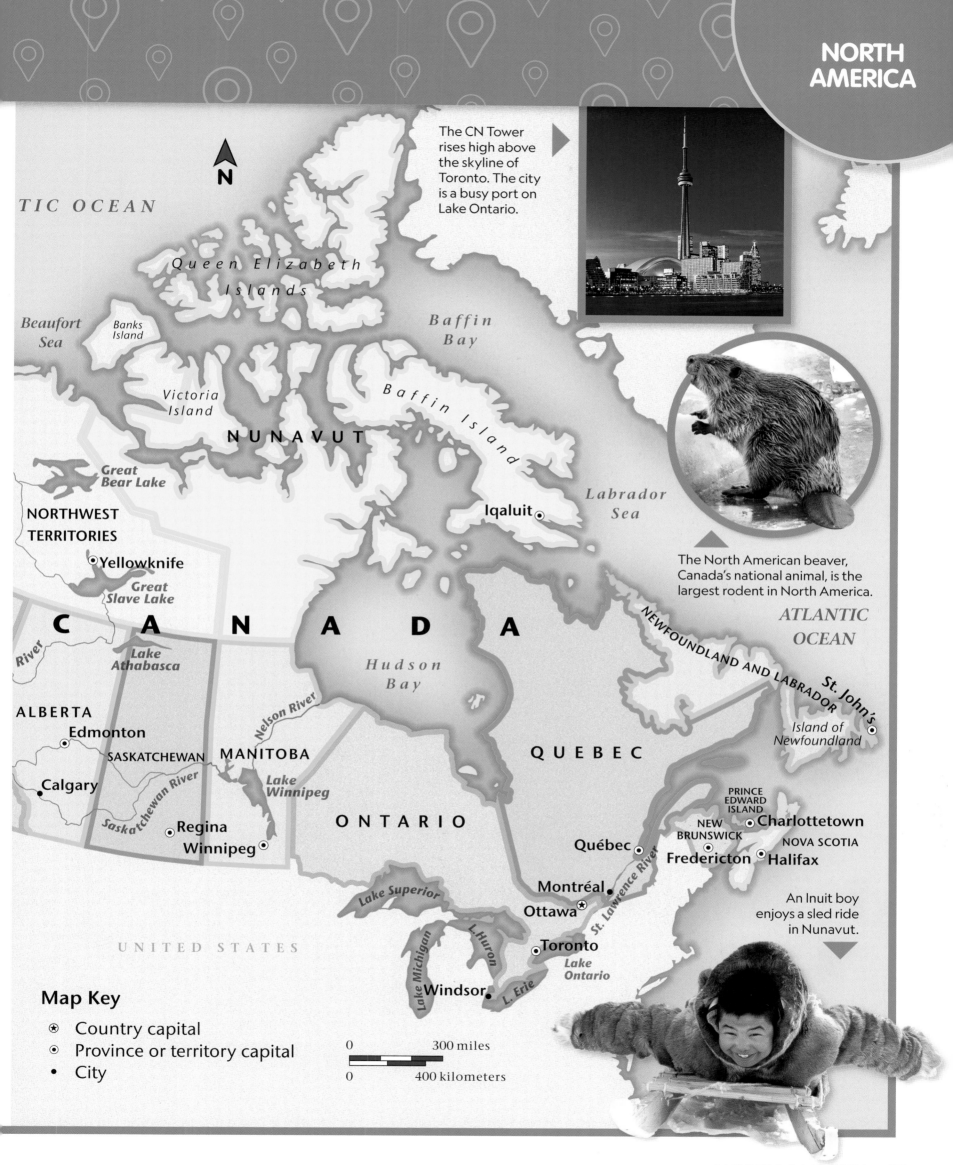

The CN Tower rises high above the skyline of Toronto. The city is a busy port on Lake Ontario.

TIC OCEAN

Queen Elizabeth Islands

Beaufort Sea

Banks Island

Baffin Bay

Victoria Island

NUNAVUT

Baffin Island

Great Bear Lake

Labrador Sea

NORTHWEST TERRITORIES

⊙ Yellowknife

Iqaluit ⊙

Great Slave Lake

The North American beaver, Canada's national animal, is the largest rodent in North America.

C A N A D A

River

ATLANTIC OCEAN

Lake Athabasca

NEWFOUNDLAND AND LABRADOR

St. John's

ALBERTA

Hudson Bay

Island of Newfoundland

Edmonton ⊙

SASKATCHEWAN

Nelson River

MANITOBA

QUEBEC

• Calgary

Saskatchewan River

Lake Winnipeg

Regina ⊙

ONTARIO

Winnipeg ⊙

PRINCE EDWARD ISLAND

Charlottetown ⊙

NEW BRUNSWICK

NOVA SCOTIA

Québec •

St. Lawrence River

Fredericton ⊙   Halifax ⊙

Lake Superior

Montréal •

Ottawa ⊛

L. Huron

An Inuit boy enjoys a sled ride in Nunavut.

Lake Michigan

• Toronto

Lake Ontario

UNITED STATES

Windsor •

L. Erie

Map Key

⊛ Country capital
⊙ Province or territory capital
• City

0   300 miles

0   400 kilometers

SOUTH AMERICA

South America is a land of many amazing things, including the world's biggest rain forest (the Amazon) and one of its driest deserts (the Atacama). It has emerald mines, mysterious ruins, and crowded modern cities. In the mountains, camel-like animals called llamas carry heavy loads. On the grasslands, cowboys called gauchos herd cattle. Foods such as potatoes and tomatoes are native to South America.

In the Amazon rain forest, a jaguar sharpens its claws on a tree trunk.

Sugarloaf Mountain rises above Guanabara Bay in Rio de Janeiro, Brazil's second most populous city.

SOUTH AMERICA

Llamas can carry 50 to 75 pounds (23 to 34 kg) up to 20 miles (32 km) a day in the Andes.

Parts of the Atacama Desert, in northern Chile, have not had rainfall in more than 100 years.

 LAND REGIONS Snowcapped mountains called the Andes run along the west coast. Rain forests and grasslands cover much of the rest of the continent. The continent's driest desert lies between the Andes and the Pacific Ocean.

 WATER The Amazon River carries more water than any other river in the world. More than 1,000 streams and rivers flow into it. Lake Titicaca is the continent's largest lake.

 CLIMATE Much of South America is warm all year. The coldest places are in the Andes and at the continent's southern tip. Each year more than 80 inches (200 cm) of rain falls in the rain forests.

 PLANTS The Amazon rain forest has more kinds of plants than any other place in the world. In the south, grasslands feed large herds of cattle and sheep.

 ANIMALS Colorful toucans, noisy howler monkeys, and giant snakes live in the rain forests. Sure-footed llamas, huge birds called condors, and guinea pigs live in the Andes. The flightless rhea, which looks like an ostrich, roams the wide southern grasslands.

The world's largest water lilies grow in the Amazon River. They are big enough to hold this young girl.

Imagine living in a place where birds are as big and as colorful as these macaws. They live in the rain forests.

Cold outside and hot inside, snow-covered volcanoes are scattered throughout the Andes.

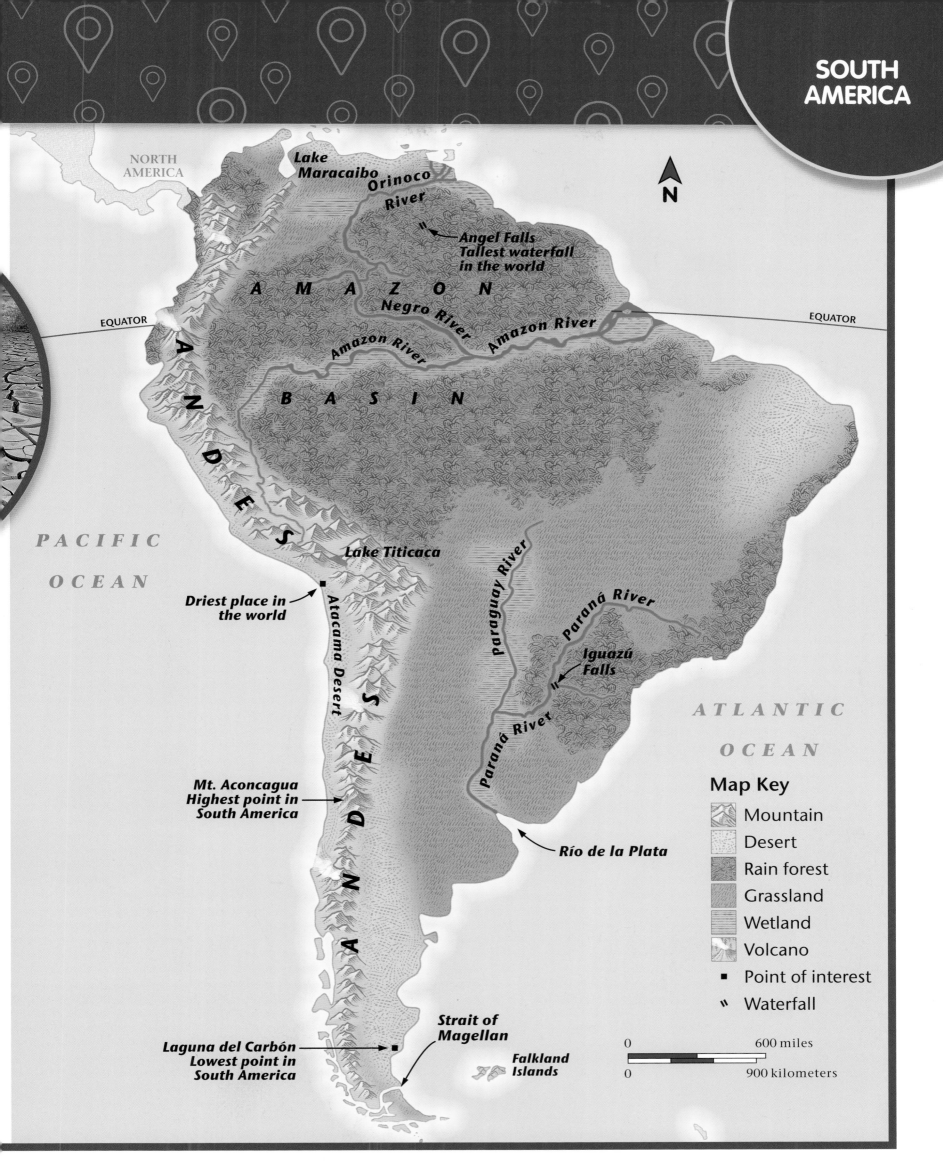

NORTH
AMERICA

Lake
Maracaibo
Orinoco
River

Angel Falls
Tallest waterfall
in the world

A M A Z O N

EQUATOR

Negro River

Amazon River

Amazon River

EQUATOR

A N D E S

B A S I N

PACIFIC

OCEAN

Lake Titicaca

Paraguay River

Paraná River

Driest place in
the world

Atacama Desert

Iguazú
Falls

Mt. Aconcagua
Highest point in
South America

A N D E S

Paraná River

ATLANTIC

OCEAN

Río de la Plata

Map Key

Mountain
Desert
Rain forest
Grassland
Wetland
Volcano
■ Point of interest
" Waterfall

Laguna del Carbón
Lowest point in
South America

Strait of
Magellan

Falkland
Islands

0   600 miles

0   900 kilometers

Many religious festivals take place all over South America. Here, a girl is dancing as she celebrates a Catholic fiesta.

This statue was carved from stone during the Tiwanaku civilization. These people lived long ago near Lake Titicaca in Bolivia.

 COUNTRIES South America has just 12 countries— French Guiana is not a country because it belongs to France. All but two of these countries border an ocean. Can you find these two landlocked countries on the map?

 CITIES Most of the largest cities are near the oceans. São Paulo, in Brazil, is South America's most populous city. Bolivia has two capital cities: La Paz and Sucre.

 PEOPLE The earliest people came from the north long ago. Colonists came from Europe, especially from Spain and Portugal. They brought African slaves to work in the fields. Most people in South America are descendants of these three groups.

 LANGUAGES Spanish and Portuguese are the continent's chief languages. Native people speak Quechua or other native languages.

This man plays his guitar to entertain people on the streets of Buenos Aires, in Argentina. Guitar music is popular in South America.

These unpolished stones are emeralds. Colombia is the top producer of these gems.

Soccer is the most popular sport in South America. This player from Brazil is focused on scoring a goal.

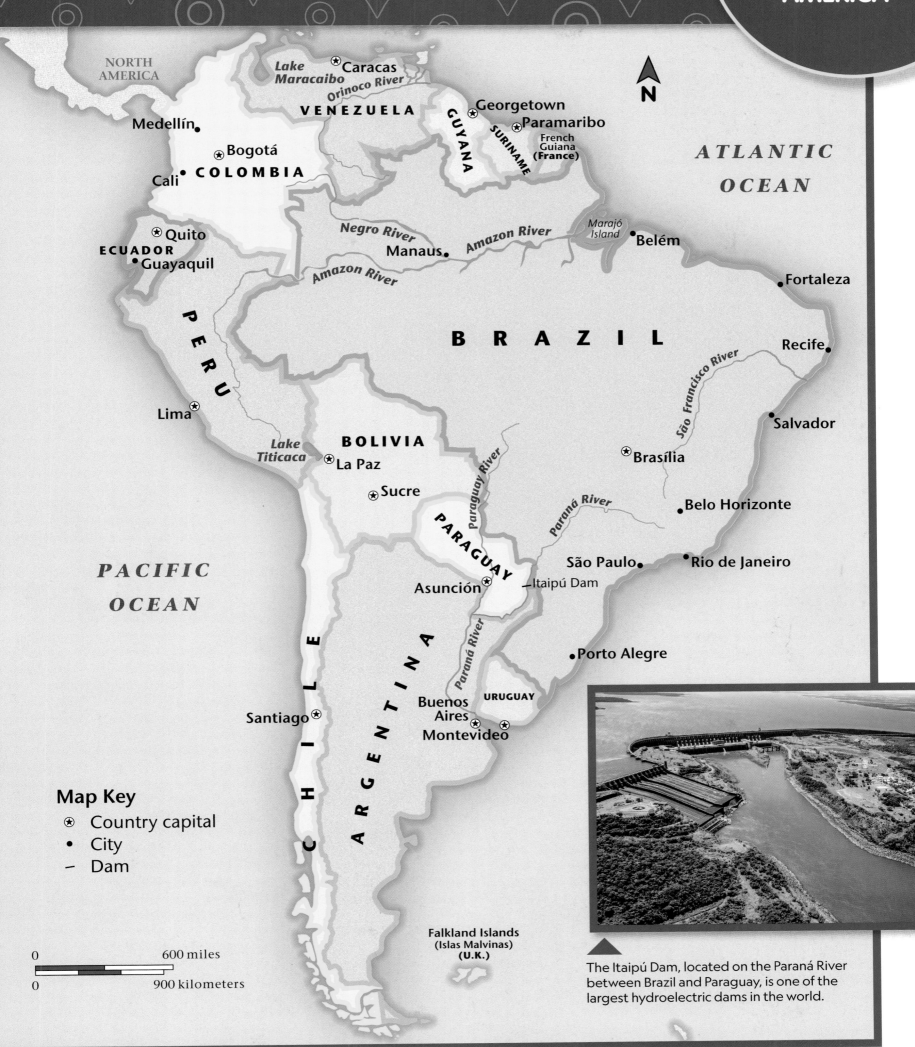

NORTH AMERICA

Lake Maracaibo ⊛ Caracas
Orinoco River
VENEZUELA
⊛ Georgetown
GUYANA
SURINAME
⊛ Paramaribo
French Guiana (France)

ATLANTIC OCEAN

Medellín •
• ⊛ Bogotá
Cali •
COLOMBIA

⊛ Quito
ECUADOR
• Guayaquil

Negro River *Amazon River*
Marajó Island
• Belém

Manaus •

Amazon River

• Fortaleza

P E R U

B R A Z I L

São Francisco River

Recife •

Lima ⊛

Lake Titicaca
BOLIVIA
⊛ La Paz

⊛ Sucre

• Salvador

⊛ Brasília

Paraguay River

PARAGUAY

Paraná River

• Belo Horizonte

PACIFIC OCEAN

São Paulo •
• Rio de Janeiro

Asunción ⊛
— Itaipú Dam

C H I L E

A R G E N T I N A

Paraná River

• Porto Alegre

URUGUAY

Buenos Aires ⊛
Montevideo ⊛

Santiago ⊛

Map Key
⊛ Country capital
• City
— Dam

0   600 miles
0   900 kilometers

Falkland Islands
(Islas Malvinas)
(U.K.)

The Itaipú Dam, located on the Paraná River between Brazil and Paraguay, is one of the largest hydroelectric dams in the world.

EUROPE

Travel through the countryside in Europe and you're likely to see castles, cuckoo clocks, and cobblestone streets. But Europe is also one of the most modern continents. You can ride one of the world's fastest trains through a tunnel beneath the English Channel, watch sports cars being made in Italy, and visit famous landmarks, such as the Eiffel Tower, in Paris. On a map, Europe may look as if it is part of Asia, but it is considered to be a separate continent.

Most puffins live in the North Atlantic Ocean near Europe, especially in the waters around Iceland. They rely on a diet of small fish.

The warm glow of sunrise lights up Hungary's Parliament Building on the bank of the Danube River in Budapest.

Farmland covers much of Europe. Fields of lavender grow in the mild climate east of the Rhône River. Perfume is made from these flowers.

Iceland

ATLANTIC OCEAN

Ireland

Great Britain

LAND REGIONS Europe's most obvious feature is its long coastline, cut with bays and peninsulas of every size. The Alps are high mountains that form a chain across a large part of southern Europe.

WATER Several large rivers flow across Europe. Some of the most important are the Danube, Rhine, and Volga.

CLIMATE Warm winds from the Atlantic Ocean help give much of Europe a mild, rainy climate. This climate makes parts of Europe good for farming.

PLANTS Europe's largest forests are in the north. Cork and olive trees grow near the Mediterranean Sea.

ANIMALS Reindeer are common in the far north. Many kinds of goatlike animals live in the Alps. Robins, nightingales, and sparrows are among Europe's native birds.

People often try to climb the Matterhorn. It is one of the highest peaks in the Alps.

PYRENEES

IBERIAN PENINSULA

M e

This is a kind of wild goat called an ibex. It is one of many kinds of hooved animals that live in the Alps and other mountainous parts of the continent.

Europe has many sandy beaches on the Mediterranean Sea. Some of the most famous are along the coasts of Italy, France, and Spain.

AFRICA

N

Norwegian Sea

SCANDINAVIAN PENINSULA

NORTHERN EUROPEAN PLAIN

U R A L   M T S.

ASIA

Volga River

North Sea

Baltic Sea

EUROPE-ASIA BOUNDARY

Caspian Sea
Lowest point
in Europe

Rhine River

CARPATHIAN MTS.

THE STEPPES

El'brus
Highest point
in Europe

Rhône River

A L P S

Matterhorn

Danube River

BALKAN MTS.

CAUCASUS MTS.

Caspian Sea

APENNINES

Black Sea

Map Key

ASIA

Sicily

Mount Etna

Mediterranean Sea

Crete

Cyprus

	Mountain
	Desert
	Coniferous forest
	Deciduous forest
	Grassland
	Wetland
	Tundra
	Volcano
——	Europe-Asia boundary

European rabbits live all over the continent.

0   600 miles

0   900 kilometers

These girls are dressed for a festival in Spain. Such celebrations keep folk traditions alive.

COUNTRIES Europe has 46 countries. Even though most of Russia is in Asia (see pages 42–43), it is usually counted as part of Europe because most of its people live there. Vatican City, Europe's smallest country, lies within the city of Rome, Italy. There are five island countries: Iceland, the United Kingdom, Ireland, Malta, and Cyprus.

CITIES Most cities in Europe are within a few hundred miles of the sea. Moscow, in Russia, is Europe's most populous city.

PEOPLE There are many different ethnic groups in Europe. More people live in cities than on farms.

LANGUAGES About 50 languages are spoken in Europe, including English, French, German, and Russian. Many Europeans speak more than one language.

The Colosseum lights up as the sun begins to set in Rome, Italy. This amphitheater was built by the Roman Empire almost 2,000 years ago.

A merchant sells cheese in a market in Ghent, Belgium. Europe is famous for its many kinds of cheese.

Reykjavík ✱ **ICELAND**

Faroe Islands (Denmark)

ATLANTIC

OCEAN

Orkney Islands

IRELAND
Dublin ✱
UNITED KINGDOM

London ✱

English Channel

Paris ✱

F R A

• Bordeaux

The euro is currently the official money in Greece and 18 other member countries of the European Union (see page 61).

PORTUGAL

✱ Lisbon

✱ Madrid

ANDORRA

S P A I N

• Seville

Balearic Islands (Spain)

Gibraltar (U.K.)

Bagpipe music is popular in Scotland, which was once an independent country. Today, Scotland is part of the United Kingdom.

N

Norwegian Sea

Shetland Islands

Map Key
⊛ Country capital
• City
☐ Disputed territory

0   600 miles
0   900 kilometers

EUROPE-ASIA BOUNDARY

ASIA

North Sea

Helsinki ⊛   • St. Petersburg

N O R W A Y

S W E D E N

F I N L A N D

Oslo ⊛
Stockholm ⊛   ⊛ Tallinn
ESTONIA

R U S S I A

DENMARK
Copenhagen ⊛   Riga ⊛
LATVIA
LITHUANIA
Kaliningrad (Russia)   ⊛ Vilnius

⊛ Moscow

Volga River

KAZAKHSTAN

NETHERLANDS
⊛ Amsterdam   • Hamburg
The Hague ⊛   Berlin ⊛
Brussels ⊛
BELGIUM
GERMANY
Rhine River
LUXEMBOURG

⊛ Minsk
B E L A R U S

Warsaw ⊛
P O L A N D

• Cracow
⊛ Kiev

Volgograd •

Prague ⊛
CZECHIA (CZECH REPUBLIC)
Danube River

U K R A I N E

NCE
Bern ⊛
SWITZERLAND   **LIECHTENSTEIN**
Rhône R.

SLOVAKIA
Vienna ⊛   ⊛ Bratislava
AUSTRIA   ⊛ Budapest
HUNGARY
SLOVENIA
Ljubljana ⊛   ⊛ Zagreb
CROATIA

MOLDOVA
Chisinau ⊛

Crimea

R O M A N I A
⊛ Bucharest

GEORGIA
Tbilisi ⊛

Caspian Sea

Baku ⊛

AZERBAIJAN

SAN MARINO
MONACO

BOSNIA AND HERZEGOVINA
Sarajevo •
Belgrade ⊛
SERBIA
Danube River

Black Sea

NOTE: The countries of Turkey, Georgia, Azerbaijan, Kazakhstan, and Russia are in both Europe and Asia.

ASIA

Corsica (France)

ITALY
MONTENEGRO
Podgorica ⊛
KOSOVO
⊛ Pristina   **BULGARIA**
⊛ Sofia

VATICAN CITY
⊛ Rome
• Naples
Tirana ⊛   ⊛ Skopje
ALBANIA   **MACEDONIA**

Istanbul •

T U R K E Y
⊛ Ankara

Sardinia (Italy)

G R E E C E

Sicily

⊛ Valletta
MALTA

⊛ Athens

Crete

⊛ Nicosia

CYPRUS

St. Basil's is a famous Russian Orthodox church. It is in Moscow, Russia's capital city.

M e d i t e r r a n e a n   S e a

AFRICA

ASIA

Asia is Earth's largest continent. Mount Everest, the world's highest mountain, is here. Asia also has some of the world's longest rivers, biggest deserts, and thickest forests. The Dead Sea is the lowest place on the continent. It is called "dead" because its water is too salty for fish and other animals to live in. More people live in Asia than anywhere else. The world's very first cities were built in river valleys in Asia long, long ago.

This endangered tiger lives in a forest reserve in India, a country where the number of tigers in the wild has been increasing in recent years.

Bright lights, colorful signs, and bustling crowds are typical of Tokyo, Japan, the most populous city in the world.

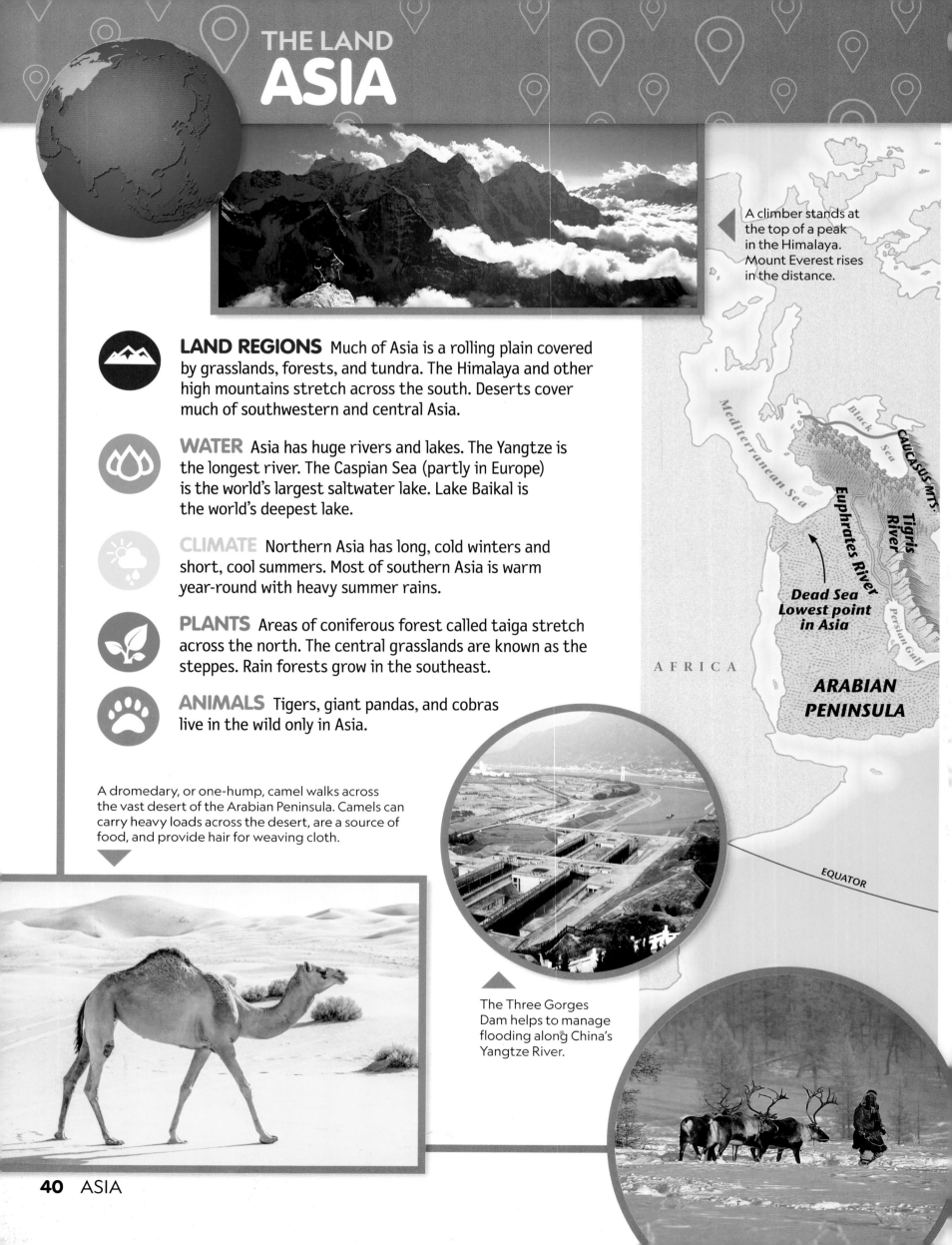

A climber stands at the top of a peak in the Himalaya. Mount Everest rises in the distance.

LAND REGIONS Much of Asia is a rolling plain covered by grasslands, forests, and tundra. The Himalaya and other high mountains stretch across the south. Deserts cover much of southwestern and central Asia.

WATER Asia has huge rivers and lakes. The Yangtze is the longest river. The Caspian Sea (partly in Europe) is the world's largest saltwater lake. Lake Baikal is the world's deepest lake.

CLIMATE Northern Asia has long, cold winters and short, cool summers. Most of southern Asia is warm year-round with heavy summer rains.

PLANTS Areas of coniferous forest called taiga stretch across the north. The central grasslands are known as the steppes. Rain forests grow in the southeast.

ANIMALS Tigers, giant pandas, and cobras live in the wild only in Asia.

A dromedary, or one-hump, camel walks across the vast desert of the Arabian Peninsula. Camels can carry heavy loads across the desert, are a source of food, and provide hair for weaving cloth.

The Three Gorges Dam helps to manage flooding along China's Yangtze River.

Mediterranean Sea

Black Sea

CAUCASUS MTS.

Euphrates River

Tigris River

Dead Sea Lowest point in Asia

Persian Gulf

AFRICA

ARABIAN PENINSULA

EQUATOR

ARCTIC OCEAN

Bering Sea

EUROPE

URAL MOUNTAINS

EUROPE-ASIA BOUNDARY

Ob River

Irtysh River

Yenisey River

Lena River

Amur River

THE STEPPES

Aral Sea

Caspian Sea

Lake Baikal
Deepest lake in the world

TIAN SHAN

GOBI

Yellow River

Indus River

HIMALAYA

Brahmaputra River

Yangtze River

Ganges River

Mt. Everest
Highest point in Asia

Mekong River

PACIFIC OCEAN

Arabian Sea

Bay of Bengal

South China Sea

New Guinea

Borneo

Sumatra

INDIAN OCEAN

Trees tower over a native village along a river in eastern Borneo. Rain forests thrive in Indonesia's warm temperatures and abundant rainfall.

0   600 miles
0   900 kilometers

Map Key

- Mountain
- Desert
- Coniferous forest
- Deciduous forest
- Rain forest
- Grassland
- Wetland
- Tundra
- Volcano
- Dry salt lake
- ─── Europe-Asia boundary

A herder leads his reindeer through the snow in northern Asia. Winters there are cold and last six to seven months.

Giant pandas live in the wild only in leafy bamboo forests that grow on mountains in southwestern China.

These are the Petronas Towers in Kuala Lumpur, Malaysia. They are the tallest twin buildings in the world.

NOTE: The countries of Russia, Kazakhstan, Azerbaijan, Georgia, and Turkey are in both Europe and Asia.

EUROPE
RUSSIA

Mediterranean Sea
Baltic
Black Sea
Istanbul
Ankara
TURKEY
GEORGIA
Tbilisi
ARMENIA
Yerevan
LEBANON
Beirut
SYRIA
Jerusalem
Damascus
ISRAEL
Amman
AZERBAIJAN
JORDAN
Baghdad
Tehran
IRAQ
I R
KUWAIT
Kuwait City
SAUDI ARABIA
BAHRAIN
Riyadh
QATAR
Doha
AFRICA
Abu Dhabi
UNITED ARAB EMIRATES
Sanaa
YEMEN
OMAN
Persian Gulf

COUNTRIES Asia has 46 countries. China is the largest country with boundaries entirely in Asia. Russia takes up the most area, but it is counted as part of Europe (see pages 36–37). Indonesia is Asia's largest island country.

CITIES Much of Asia is too high, too dry, or too cold for people to live in. Most cities are near the coast or along busy rivers. Tokyo, in Japan, is the most populous city.

PEOPLE Asia has more people than any other continent. Each ethnic group has its own language, customs, and appearance. Many people are farmers, but others work in high-tech industries.

LANGUAGES More than 2,300 languages are spoken by the people of Asia—the most of any continent. Chinese has more native speakers than any other language.

This young boy works in a spice market. In India people mix lots of spices together to make a strong flavor called curry.

This masked dancer is from Bali, one of more than 3,000 islands that make up the country of Indonesia.

This boy in Shanghai, China, draws symbols used in writing the Chinese language. Each symbol stands for a word or an idea.

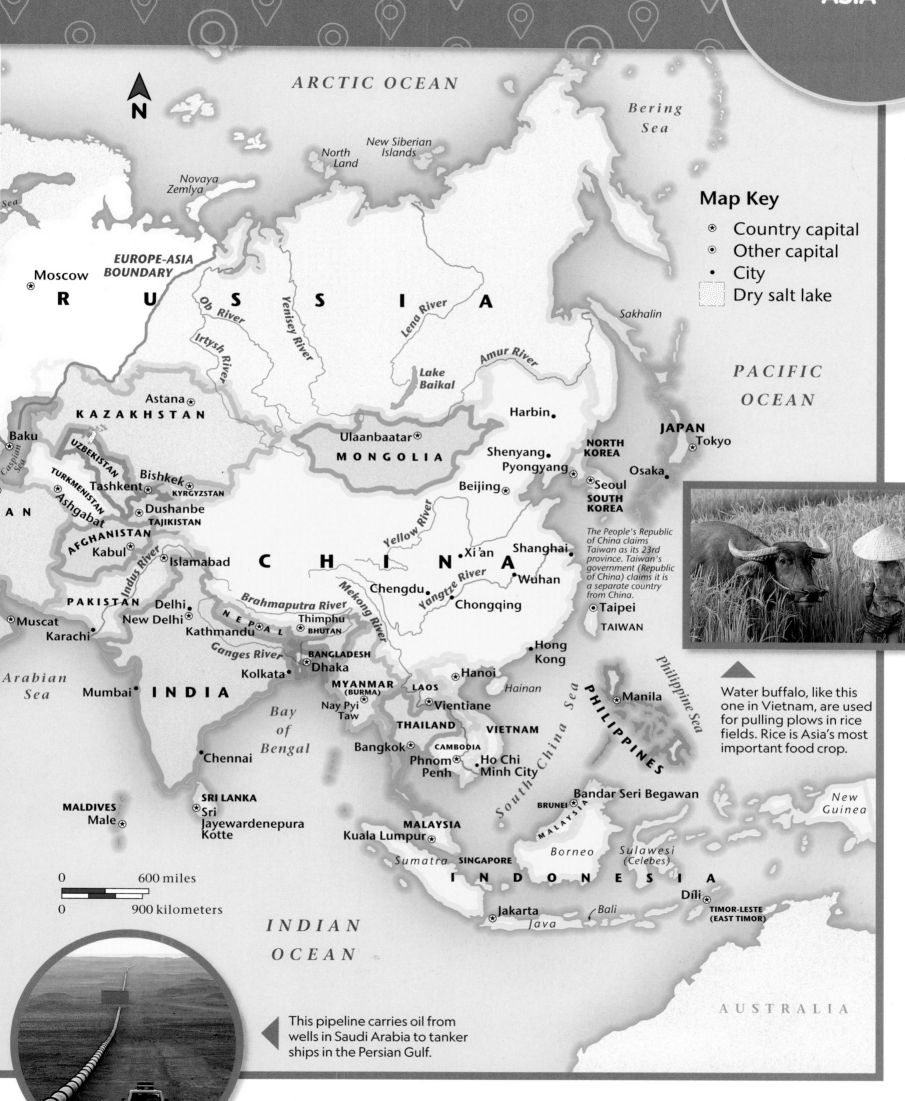

ARCTIC OCEAN

Bering Sea

North Land

New Siberian Islands

Novaya Zemlya

Sea

N

Map Key
- ⊛ Country capital
- ⊙ Other capital
- • City
- ▦ Dry salt lake

EUROPE-ASIA BOUNDARY

⊛ Moscow

R   U   S   S   I   A

Ob River

Irtysh River

Yenisey River

Lena River

Amur River

Lake Baikal

Sakhalin

PACIFIC OCEAN

Astana ⊛

K A Z A K H S T A N

⊛ Ulaanbaatar

M O N G O L I A

Harbin •

Shenyang •

⊙ Pyongyang

JAPAN
• Tokyo

⊛ Baku

Caspian Sea

UZBEKISTAN

TURKMENISTAN

Tashkent ⊛

Bishkek ⊙

KYRGYZSTAN

NORTH KOREA

Osaka •

⊛ Ashgabat

⊛ Dushanbe

TAJIKISTAN

⊛ Seoul

SOUTH KOREA

Beijing ⊛

AFGHANISTAN

Kabul ⊛

Indus River

⊙ Islamabad

C   H   I   N   A

Yellow River

Xi'an •

Shanghai •

The People's Republic of China claims Taiwan as its 23rd province. Taiwan's government (Republic of China) claims it is a separate country from China.

PAKISTAN

Delhi •

⊛ New Delhi

Brahmaputra River

NEPAL

Thimphu ⊙

⊛ Muscat

Karachi •

⊛ Kathmandu

BHUTAN

Ganges River

Chengdu •

Yangtze River

Wuhan •

Mekong River

Chongqing •

⊙ Taipei

TAIWAN

Hong Kong •

⊛ Dhaka

BANGLADESH

Kolkata •

Hanoi ⊙

Arabian Sea

Mumbai •

I N D I A

MYANMAR (BURMA)

Nay Pyi Taw ⊙

LAOS

⊙ Vientiane

Hainan

Philippine Sea

Manila ⊛

P H I L I P P I N E S

South China Sea

Bay of Bengal

THAILAND

VIETNAM

Chennai •

Bangkok ⊛

CAMBODIA

Phnom ⊛ Penh

Ho Chi • Minh City

MALDIVES
Male ⊛

SRI LANKA

⊛ Sri Jayewardenepura Kotte

Bandar Seri Begawan

BRUNEI

New Guinea

MALAYSIA

MALAYSIA

Kuala Lumpur ⊛

Borneo

Sulawesi (Celebes)

Sumatra

SINGAPORE

I N D O N E S I A

0   600 miles
0   900 kilometers

⊛ Jakarta

Java

Bali

Díli ⊙

TIMOR-LESTE (EAST TIMOR)

INDIAN OCEAN

AUSTRALIA

▲ Water buffalo, like this one in Vietnam, are used for pulling plows in rice fields. Rice is Asia's most important food crop.

◀ This pipeline carries oil from wells in Saudi Arabia to tanker ships in the Persian Gulf.

AFRICA

Elephants, lions, gorillas, hippopotamuses, giraffes, and zebras are among the amazing animals you can see in Africa's parks, plains, forests, and mountains. You can also visit a busy, modern city such as Nairobi, in Kenya; shop in colorful, outdoor markets; and see how diamonds are mined in South Africa. You can even take a sailboat ride past ancient temples along the Nile and climb some of the world's highest sand dunes in Earth's biggest hot desert—the Sahara.

African elephants roam the continent's grasslands. They are Earth's largest land animal.

Buildings in Ouarzazate, Morocco, are an example of the traditional Arab architecture found in northern Africa.

Acacia trees are common in the African savanna. The trees send roots down as far as 200 feet (61 m) to reach water sources beneath the dry grasslands.

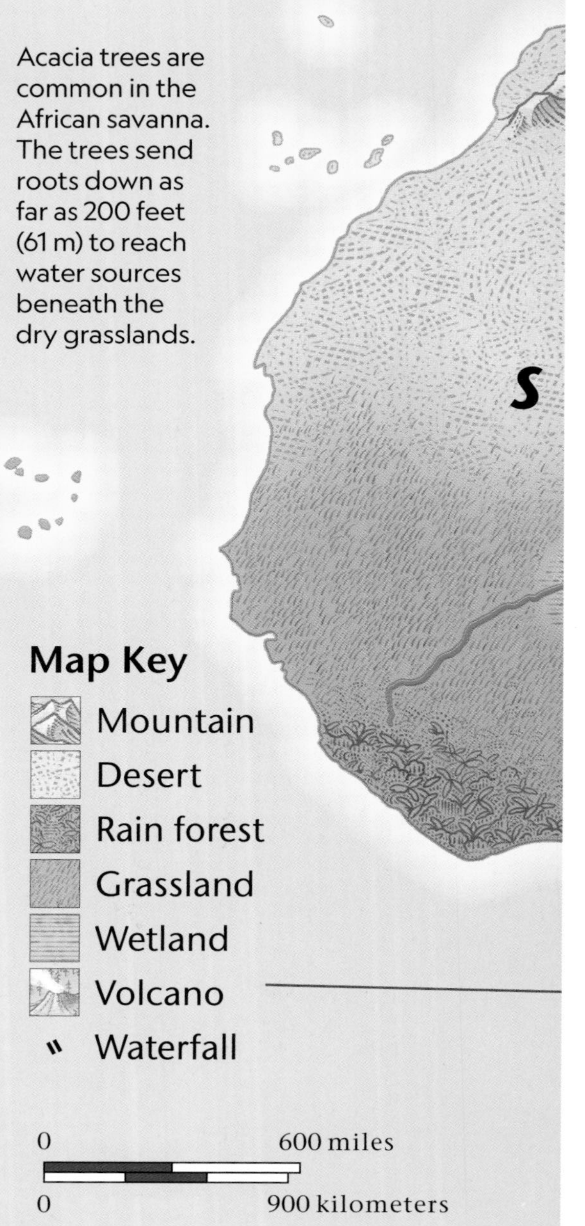

S

LAND REGIONS Most of Africa is a high, flat plateau. There are few mountains. The Sahara and the Kalahari are its largest deserts. Rain forests grow along the Equator. Grasslands, called savannas, cover much of the rest of the continent.

WATER The Nile and the Congo are Africa's longest rivers. Most of Africa's largest lakes are in the Great Rift Valley.

CLIMATE The Equator crosses Africa's middle, so many places on the continent are hot. It is always wet in the rain forests. Much of the rest of Africa has wet and dry seasons.

PLANTS Thorny trees called acacias provide food and shade for grassland animals. Date palms grow around desert water holes. Mahogany is one of many kinds of rain forest trees.

ANIMALS Some of Africa's most familiar animals are shown here. There are also lions and many kinds of antelopes. Lemurs live on Madagascar, Africa's largest island.

Map Key

- Mountain
- Desert
- Rain forest
- Grassland
- Wetland
- Volcano
- Waterfall

0	600 miles
0	900 kilometers

Victoria Falls, on the Zambezi River, is one of Africa's wonders. Its African name means "smoke that thunders."

Giraffes are the world's tallest animal. They can tower above trees that grow on grasslands.

Sand dunes in the Sahara rise high above this all-terrain vehicle. This huge desert covers most of northern Africa.

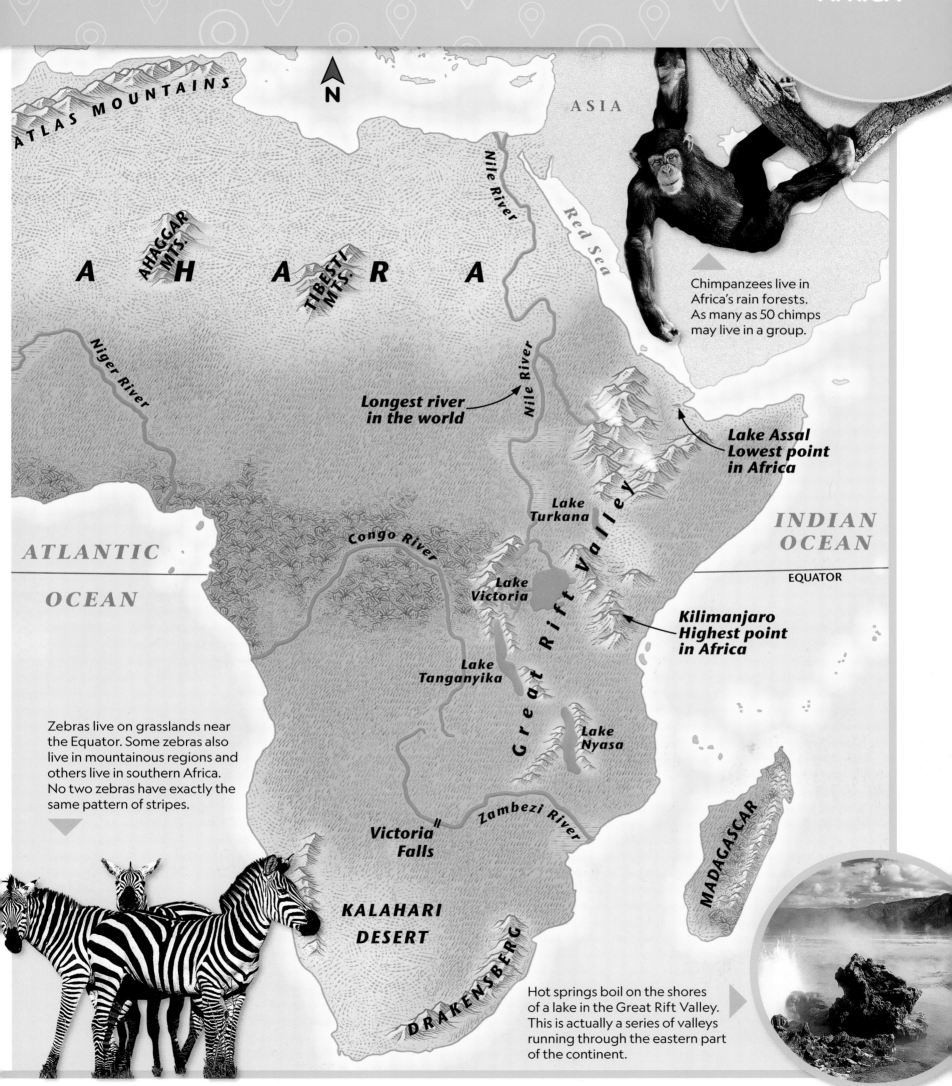

ATLAS MOUNTAINS

N

ASIA

AHAGGAR MTS.

TIBESTI MTS.

S A H A R A

Niger River

Nile River

Red Sea

Chimpanzees live in Africa's rain forests. As many as 50 chimps may live in a group.

Longest river in the world

Nile River

Lake Assal Lowest point in Africa

Congo River

Lake Turkana

INDIAN OCEAN

ATLANTIC

OCEAN

Lake Victoria

Great Rift Valley

EQUATOR

Kilimanjaro Highest point in Africa

Zebras live on grasslands near the Equator. Some zebras also live in mountainous regions and others live in southern Africa. No two zebras have exactly the same pattern of stripes.

Lake Tanganyika

Lake Nyasa

Zambezi River

MADAGASCAR

Victoria Falls

KALAHARI DESERT

DRAKENSBERG

Hot springs boil on the shores of a lake in the Great Rift Valley. This is actually a series of valleys running through the eastern part of the continent.

THE PEOPLE
AFRICA

Small sailboats called feluccas carry trade goods along the Nile. The river flows north out of Lake Victoria.

COUNTRIES Much of Africa was ruled by European countries from the late 1800s to the mid 1900s. Today, there are 54 independent countries. Algeria has the most land. Nigeria has the most people.

CITIES Cairo and Lagos are Africa's most populous cities. Both are busy port cities and centers of trade. But many people live in villages and on farms rather than in cities.

PEOPLE Most people in northern Africa are Arabic-speaking Muslims. Most black Africans living south of the Sahara belong to hundreds of different ethnic groups. Many Europeans live in major cities and in South Africa.

LANGUAGES Arabic is spoken in northern Africa. Native languages are spoken south of the Sahara. English, French, and Portuguese are the main European languages.

Casablanca

Canary Islands (Spain)

WESTERN SAHARA (Morocco)

MAURITANIA

Nouakchott

CABO VERDE

★ Praia   Dakar   SENEGAL

Banjul ★

GAMBIA   Bamako
Bissau ★ GUINEA-   ★
         BISSAU
              GUINEA

Conakry ★ Yamoussoukro ★

Freetown ★

SIERRA LEONE   LIBERIA

Monrovia ★

CÔTE D'IVOIRE (IVORY COAST)

These students in Kenya study many of the same subjects you do. Their classes are taught in English.

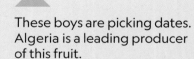

These boys are picking dates. Algeria is a leading producer of this fruit.

The Sphinx and the pyramid behind it were built by people who lived in Egypt thousands of years ago.

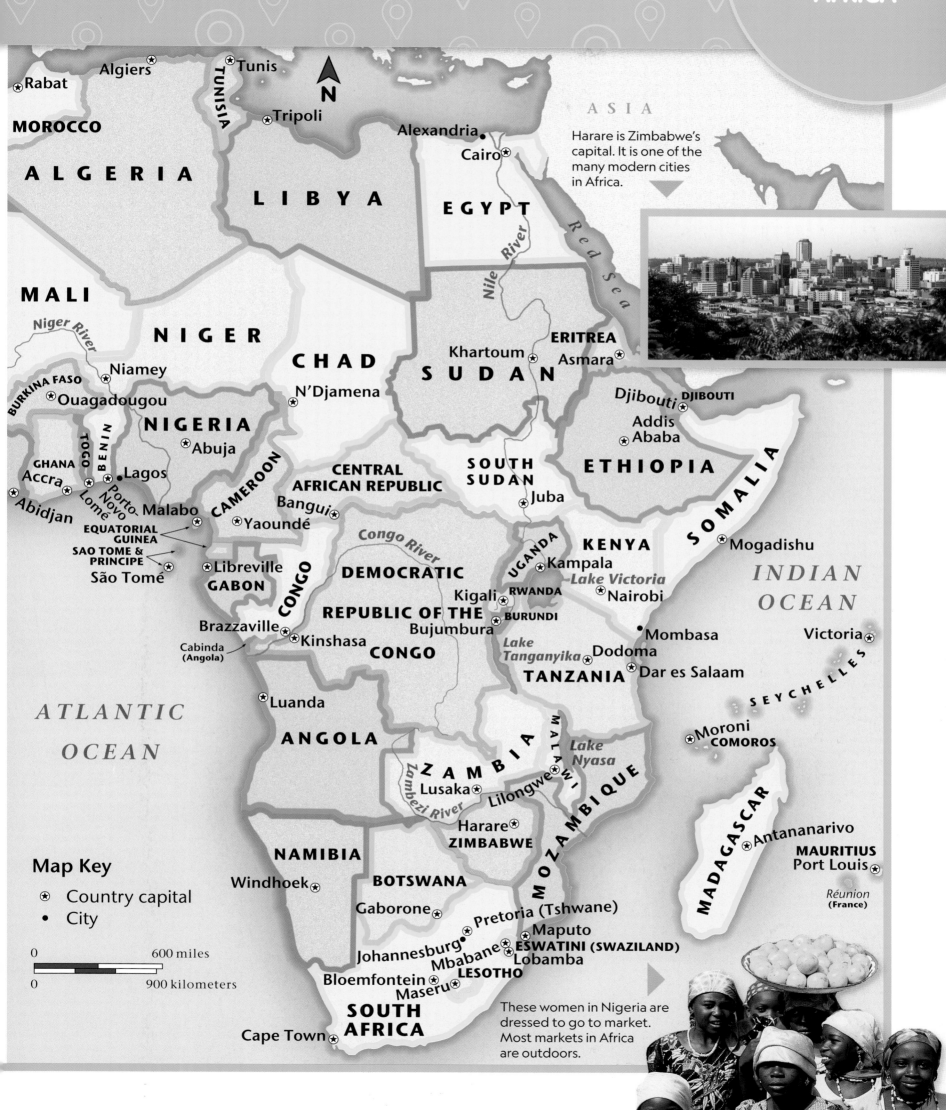

Rabat
MOROCCO
Algiers
Tunis
TUNISIA
Tripoli

N

ALGERIA
LIBYA
Alexandria
Cairo
EGYPT

ASIA

Harare is Zimbabwe's capital. It is one of the many modern cities in Africa.

MALI

Niger River

NIGER
CHAD
N'Djamena

Red Sea

Nile River

Khartoum
SUDAN
Asmara
ERITREA
Djibouti DJIBOUTI
Addis Ababa

BURKINA FASO
Niamey
Ouagadougou
NIGERIA
Abuja
BENIN
TOGO
GHANA
Accra
Lagos
Porto Novo
Lomé
Abidjan
Malabo
EQUATORIAL GUINEA
SAO TOME & PRINCIPE
São Tomé
CAMEROON
Yaoundé
Bangui
CENTRAL AFRICAN REPUBLIC
SOUTH SUDAN
Juba
ETHIOPIA
SOMALIA
Mogadishu

INDIAN OCEAN

Libreville
GABON
CONGO
Brazzaville
Cabinda (Angola)
Kinshasa
DEMOCRATIC REPUBLIC OF THE
CONGO
Congo River
Kigali
Bujumbura
UGANDA
Kampala
RWANDA
BURUNDI
Lake Victoria
Nairobi
KENYA

ATLANTIC OCEAN

Luanda
ANGOLA

Lake Tanganyika
Mombasa
Dodoma
Dar es Salaam
TANZANIA

Victoria
SEYCHELLES

Moroni
COMOROS

ZAMBIA
Lusaka
MALAWI
Lake Nyasa
Lilongwe
Zambezi River
Harare
ZIMBABWE
MOZAMBIQUE

MADAGASCAR
Antananarivo
MAURITIUS
Port Louis

Réunion (France)

NAMIBIA
Windhoek
BOTSWANA
Gaborone
Pretoria (Tshwane)
Johannesburg
Maputo
ESWATINI (SWAZILAND)
Mbabane
Lobamba
LESOTHO
Bloemfontein
Maseru
SOUTH AFRICA
Cape Town

Map Key
⊛ Country capital
• City

0   600 miles
0   900 kilometers

These women in Nigeria are dressed to go to market. Most markets in Africa are outdoors.

AUSTRALIA

Australia is an unusual place. It is Earth's smallest and flattest continent and one of the driest, too. "Aussies," as Australians refer to themselves, call their continent the "land down under" because the entire continent lies south of, or "under," the Equator. Most Australians live in cities along the coast. But Australia also has huge cattle and sheep ranches. Many ranch children live far from school. They get their lessons by mail or from the internet. Their doctors even visit by airplane!

Kangaroos live in the wild only in Australia. They live in groups called mobs.

The Sydney Opera House is recognized worldwide for its unique design.

AUSTRALIA

The "Three Sisters" rock formation is a stunning site in the Blue Mountains of Australia. These mountains are part of the Great Dividing Range.

INDIAN OCEAN

A sign warns drivers to look out for kangaroos. The red rock formation, called Uluṟu by Aboriginals and Ayers Rock by others, is in the Western Plateau.

Hamersley Range

Darling Range

LAND REGIONS The Great Dividing Range stretches through eastern Australia and into Tasmania. Most of the rest of Australia is a plateau covered by grasslands and deserts.

WATER The Darling, Australia's longest river, is dry during part of the year. So is Lake Eyre, the continent's largest lake. Water lies underground in the Great Artesian Basin.

CLIMATE Much of the continent is very dry. Winds called monsoons bring heavy seasonal rains to the northern coast. Southern Australia can be cold in winter, but much of the continent is warm year-round.

PLANTS Eucalyptus, or gum, trees and acacias are the most common kinds of plants. They grow throughout much of Australia.

ANIMALS Australia has many unusual mammals. Female koalas and kangaroos raise their young in pouches on their bellies. The platypus is a mammal that has a bill like a duck's. Its babies hatch from eggs.

Moss covers trees and logs in a forest in Tasmania. This island has a much wetter climate than most of mainland Australia.

The cackling laugh of the kookaburra is a familiar forest sound.

Map Key

- Mountain
- Desert
- Deciduous forest
- Rain forest
- Grassland
- Wetland
- Dry salt lake
- Reef
- ■ Point of interest

Coral
Sea

Gulf of
Carpentaria

Kimberley
Plateau

**Longest coral
reef system
in the world**

Great Barrier Reef

WESTERN

GREAT DIVIDING RANGE

MacDonnell Ranges

PLATEAU

Uluru
(Ayers Rock)

GREAT
ARTESIAN
BASIN

Lake Eyre
**Lowest point
in Australia**

Flinders Ranges

Darling River

Mt. Kosciuszko
**Highest point
in Australia**

Murray River

Great Australian Bight

Limestone towers
rise above a desert
in Western Australia.
Desert covers much
of the continent.

Bass
Strait

Koalas live only in
eucalyptus trees.
At one time koalas
almost became
extinct. Now they
are protected
by strict laws.

Tasmania

| 0 | | | 600 miles |
| 0 | | | 900 kilometers |

AUSTRALIA

Surfing is popular in Australia. There is even a suburb of Queensland's Gold Coast named Surfers Paradise.

INDIAN OCEAN

• **Port Hedland**

WESTERN AUSTRALIA

COUNTRIES Australia is the only continent that is also a country. It is divided into six states plus the Northern and Australian Capital territories.

CITIES All the chief cities are near the coast except the capital, Canberra, which is almost 100 miles (160 km) inland. Sydney has the most people, followed by Melbourne, Brisbane, and Perth.

PEOPLE Most Australians are descendants of settlers from the United Kingdom and Ireland. Aboriginals came to Australia from Asia some 40,000 years ago.

LANGUAGES English is the main language of Australia. Aboriginals speak some 250 different languages.

⊙ **Perth**

The world's largest cultured pearls are grown in oyster beds along Australia's northern coast.

Cafés can be hundreds of miles apart in the outback, a dry, remote, and largely uninhabited region.

This Aboriginal is playing a wooden pipe called a didgeridoo. Many of Australia's native people live in the Northern Territory.

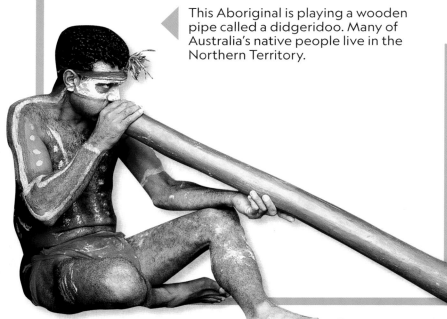

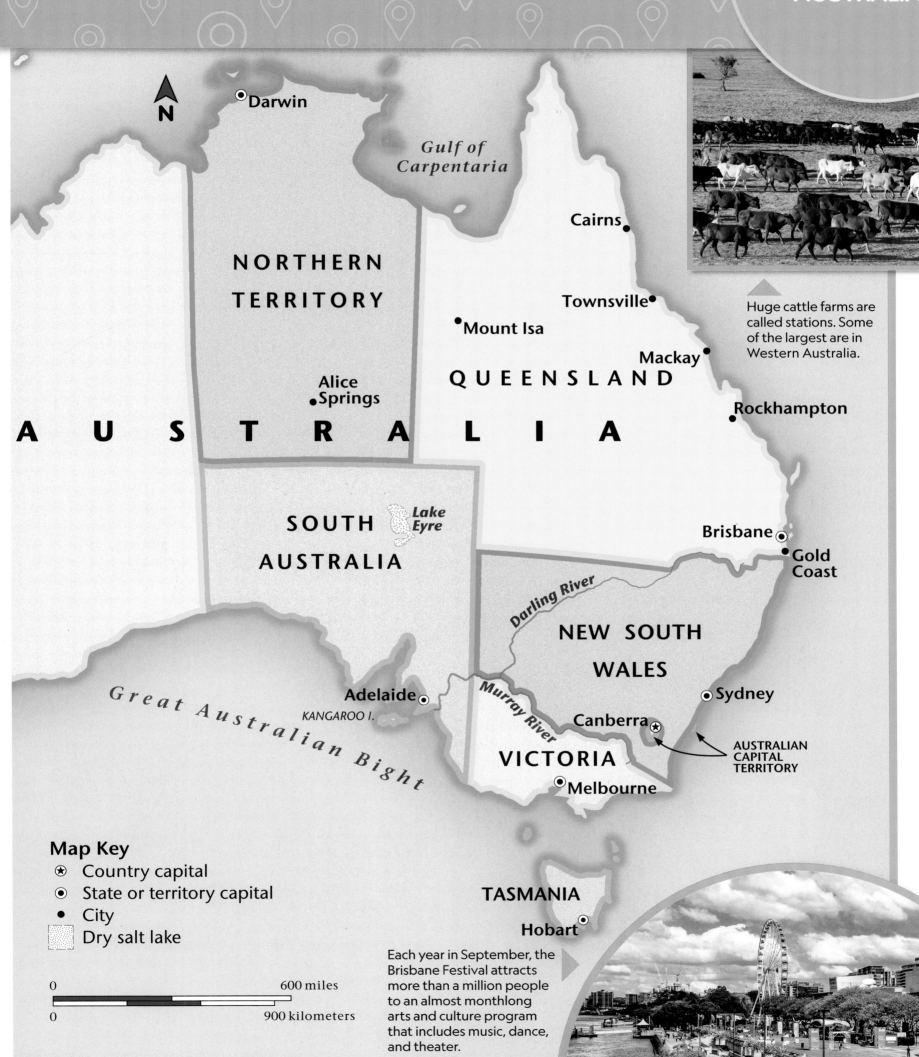

N

Darwin

*Gulf of
Carpentaria*

NORTHERN

TERRITORY

Cairns

Townsville

Mount Isa

Mackay

QUEENSLAND

Alice
Springs

A U S T R A L I A

Rockhampton

SOUTH

*Lake
Eyre*

AUSTRALIA

Brisbane

Gold
Coast

Darling River

NEW SOUTH

WALES

Sydney

G r e a t   A u s t r a l i a n   B i g h t

Adelaide

KANGAROO I.

Murray River

Canberra

AUSTRALIAN
CAPITAL
TERRITORY

VICTORIA

Melbourne

Huge cattle farms are
called stations. Some
of the largest are in
Western Australia.

Map Key
⊛ Country capital
⊙ State or territory capital
• City
▦ Dry salt lake

TASMANIA

Hobart

Each year in September, the
Brisbane Festival attracts
more than a million people
to an almost monthlong
arts and culture program
that includes music, dance,
and theater.

0			600 miles

0			900 kilometers

ANTARCTICA

*B*rrrr! Antarctica takes first place as the coldest continent. It is the land around the South Pole. An ice sheet two miles (3 km) thick in places covers most of the land. Temperatures rarely get above freezing. It is also the only continent that has no countries. It has research stations but no cities. The only people are scientists, explorers, and tourists. Everyone stays for a while, then goes home. The largest land animals that live here year-round are a few kinds of insects!

Antarctica's deep-diving Weddell seals can stay underwater 45 minutes as they hunt for fish.

Water temperatures around Antarctica range from 28°F to 50°F (-2°C to 10°C). Whales and other sea animals inhabit these cold waters all or part of each year.

This strong-sided ship is an icebreaker. It cuts a path through ice in the Ross Sea.

LAND REGIONS The Transantarctic Mountains divide the continent into two parts. East Antarctica, where the South Pole is located, is mostly a high, flat, icy area. West Antarctica is mountainous. The Antarctic Peninsula extends like a finger toward South America. Vinson Massif is the highest peak.

WATER Most of Earth's freshwater is frozen in Antarctica's ice sheet. The ice breaks off when it meets the sea. These huge floating chunks of ice in the ocean are called icebergs.

CLIMATE Antarctica is cold, windy, and dry. What little snow falls turns to ice. The thick ice sheet has built up over millions of years.

PLANTS Billions of tiny plants live in the surrounding oceans. Mosses and lichens grow on exposed rocks.

ANIMALS Penguins and other seabirds nest on the coast. Whales, seals, and tiny shrimplike krill live in the oceans.

Jellyfish grow very large under the sea ice around the continent. Here they have few enemies so they live a long time.

ATLANTIC OCEAN

ANTARCTIC CIRCLE

ANTARCTIC

Scientists, including those at Argentina's Brown Station, spend months studying changes in Earth's environment.

Bellingshausen Sea

ELLSWORTH LAND

Amundsen Sea

Adélie penguins live in large colonies along the shores of Antarctica and nearby islands. They feed mainly on fish and krill.

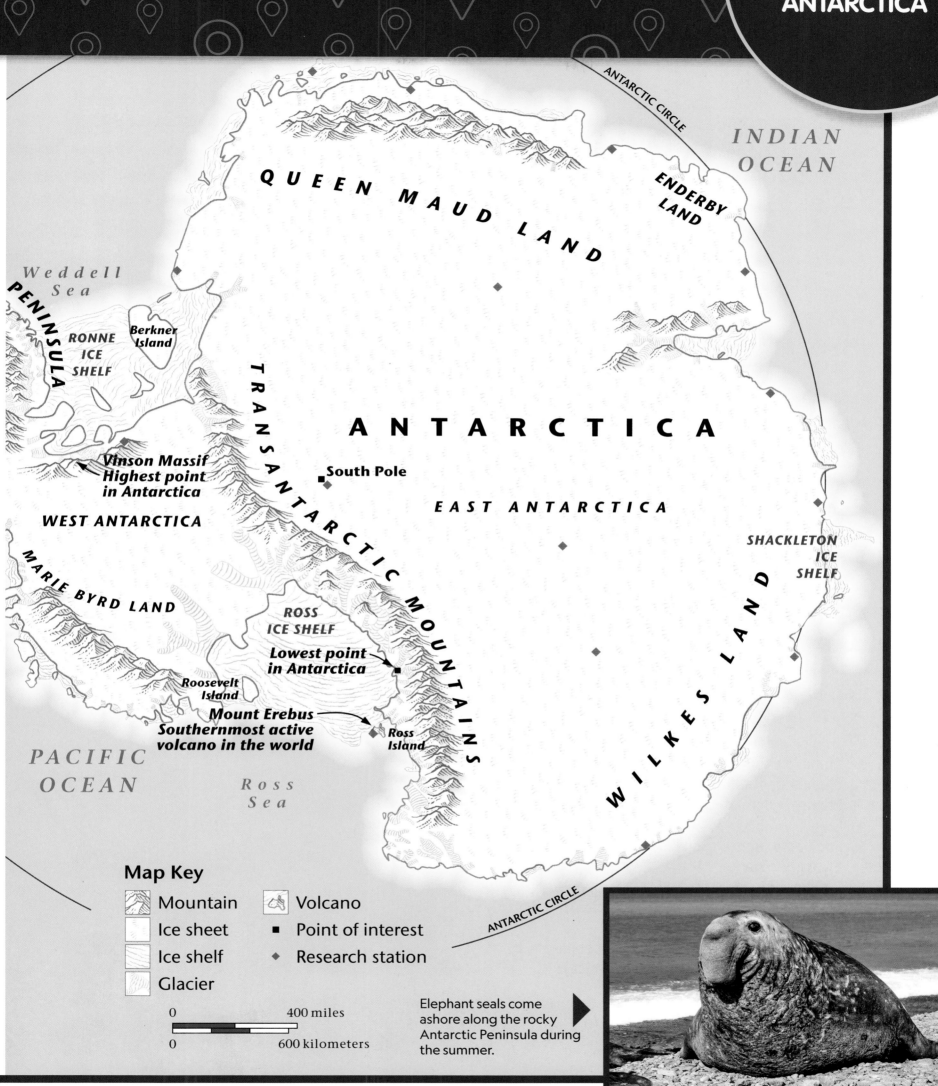

INDIAN OCEAN

ANTARCTIC CIRCLE

QUEEN MAUD LAND

ENDERBY LAND

Weddell Sea

PENINSULA

RONNE ICE SHELF

Berkner Island

ANTARCTICA

TRANSANTARCTIC MOUNTAINS

Vinson Massif Highest point in Antarctica

WEST ANTARCTICA

South Pole

EAST ANTARCTICA

SHACKLETON ICE SHELF

MARIE BYRD LAND

ROSS ICE SHELF

Lowest point in Antarctica

Roosevelt Island

Mount Erebus Southernmost active volcano in the world

Ross Island

WILKES LAND

PACIFIC OCEAN

Ross Sea

ANTARCTIC CIRCLE

Map Key

Mountain
Ice sheet
Ice shelf
Glacier

Volcano
Point of interest
Research station

0   400 miles
0   600 kilometers

Elephant seals come ashore along the rocky Antarctic Peninsula during the summer.

WORLD AT A GLANCE

Land

The Continents, Largest to Smallest

1. **Asia:** 17,208,000 sq mi (44,570,000 sq km)
2. **Africa:** 11,608,000 sq mi (30,065,000 sq km)
3. **North America:** 9,449,000 sq mi (24,474,000 sq km)
4. **South America:** 6,880,000 sq mi (17,819,000 sq km)
5. **Antarctica:** 5,100,000 sq mi (13,209,000 sq km)
6. **Europe:** 3,841,000 sq mi (9,947,000 sq km)
7. **Australia:** 2,989,000 sq mi (7,741,000 sq km)

People

More than 7.5 billion people live on Earth in almost 200 countries. More than half of the world's people live in Asia. A little more than half of the global population lives in towns and cities.

Five Largest Countries by Number of People (2017 data)

1. **China, Asia:** 1,379,303,000 people
2. **India, Asia:** 1,281,936,000 people
3. **United States, North America:** 326,626,000 people
4. **Indonesia, Asia:** 260,581,000 people
5. **Brazil, South America:** 207,353,000 people

Ten Largest Cities* by Number of People (2016 data)

1. **Tokyo, Japan (Asia):** 38,140,000 people
2. **Delhi, India (Asia):** 26,454,000 people
3. **Shanghai, China (Asia):** 24,484,000
4. **Mumbai (Bombay), India (Asia):** 21,357,000 people
5. **São Paulo, Brazil (South America):** 21,297,000 people
6. **Beijing, China (Asia):** 21,240,000 people
7. **Mexico City, Mexico (North America):** 21,157,000 people
8. **Cairo, Egypt (Africa):** 19,128,000 people
9. **New York City, U.S.A. (North America):** 18,604,000 people
10. **Dhaka, Bangladesh (Asia):** 18,237,000 people

*Figures are for metropolitan areas

Water

The Oceans, Largest to Smallest

1. **Pacific Ocean:** 69,000,000 sq mi (178,800,000 sq km)
2. **Atlantic Ocean:** 35,400,000 sq mi (91,700,000 sq km)
3. **Indian Ocean:** 29,400,000 sq mi (76,200,000 sq km)
4. **Arctic Ocean:** 5,600,000 sq mi (14,700,000 sq km)

Highest, Tallest, Longest, Largest

The numbers below show locations on the map.

1 **Highest Mountain on a Continent**
Mt. Everest, in Asia: 29,035 ft (8,850 m)

2 **Tallest Waterfall**
Angel Falls, in South America: 3,212 ft (979 m)

3 **Largest Island**
Greenland, borders the Arctic and Atlantic Oceans: 836,000 sq mi (2,166,000 sq km)

4 **Largest Ocean**
Pacific Ocean: 69,000,000 sq mi (178,800,000 sq km)

5 **Longest River**
Nile River, in Africa: 4,400 mi (7,081 km)

6 **Largest Freshwater Lake**
Lake Superior, in North America: 31,700 sq mi (82,100 sq km)

7 **Largest Saltwater Lake**
Caspian Sea, in Europe-Asia: 143,200 sq mi (371,000 sq km)

8 **Longest Coral Reef System**
Great Barrier Reef, in Australia: 1,429 miles (2,300 km)

9 **Largest Hot Desert**
Sahara, in Africa: 3,475,000 sq mi (9,000,000 sq km)

10 **Largest Cold Desert**
Antarctica: 5,100,000 sq mi (13,209,000 sq km)

GLOSSARY

Arab people living in the Arabian Peninsula of southwestern Asia or in northern Africa who are linked by language and culture

capital city the seat of government for a country, state, or province

city a settled place where people work in jobs other than farming

colonist a person who settles in a new place, often to claim land for another country

coral reef a stony formation in warm, shallow ocean water that is made up of the skeletons of tiny sea animals called corals

country a place that has boundaries, a name, a flag, and a government that is the highest world authority over the land and the people who live there

environment the world around you, including people, cities, plants and animals, air, water—everything

ethnic group people who share a common ancestry, language, beliefs, and traditions

euro the official currency of the European Union

European Union an organization of 28 European countries (Austria,* Belgium,* Bulgaria, Croatia, Cyprus,* Czechia [Czech Republic], Denmark, Estonia,* Finland,* France,* Germany,* Greece,* Hungary, Ireland,* Italy,* Latvia,* Lithuania,* Luxembourg,* Malta,* Netherlands,* Poland, Portugal,* Romania, Slovakia,* Slovenia,* Spain,* Sweden, and United Kingdom) as of July 2018. Countries marked with an asterisk (*) use the euro as their official currency.

glacier a large, slow-moving mass of ice. Glaciers that cover huge areas are called ice sheets, or continental glaciers

hydroelectric a type of electricity made by harnessing the energy of running water

lemur a mammal that is a kind of primate living in the wild only on Madagascar and other nearby African islands. Most kinds of lemurs are endangered.

lichen a plantlike organism that is part alga and part fungus and that usually lives where few plants can survive

mosses nonflowering, low-growing green plants that grow on rocks and trees

Muslim a person who practices Islam, a religion that has more than two billion followers

outback the dry interior region of Australia where few people live

plains large areas of mainly flat land often covered with grasses

plateau a large, mainly level area of high land

province a unit of government similar to a state

state a unit of government that takes up a specific area within a country, as in one of the 50 large political units in the United States

steppe a Russian word for the grasslands that stretch from eastern Europe into Asia

taiga a Russian word for the scattered coniferous forests that grow in cold, northern regions

tributary a river or stream that flows into a larger river

West Indies a chain of islands stretching from the Bahamas to the northern coast of Venezuela that separates the Gulf of Mexico and the Caribbean Sea from the Atlantic Ocean.

METRIC CONVERSIONS FOUND IN THIS ATLAS

CONVERSIONS TO METRIC MEASUREMENTS

WHEN YOU KNOW	MULTIPLY BY	TO FIND
INCHES (IN)	2.54	CENTIMETERS (CM)
FEET (FT)	0.30	METERS (M)
MILES (MI)	1.61	KILOMETERS (KM)
SQUARE MILES (SQ MI)	2.59	SQUARE KILOMETERS (SQ KM)
POUNDS (LB)	0.45	KILOGRAMS (KG)

CONVERSIONS FROM METRIC MEASUREMENTS

WHEN YOU KNOW	MULTIPLY BY	TO FIND
CENTIMETERS (CM)	0.39	INCHES (IN)
METERS (M)	3.28	FEET (FT)
KILOMETERS (KM)	0.62	MILES (MI)
SQUARE KILOMETERS (SQ KM)	0.39	SQUARE MILES (SQ MI)
KILOGRAMS (KG)	2.20	POUNDS (LB)

INDEX

Pictures and the text that describes them have their page numbers printed in **bold** type.

There's always more ...
TO EXPLORE!

National Geographic Kids has the perfect atlas for kids of every age, from preschool through high school—all with the latest age-appropriate facts, maps, images, and more.

The atlas series is designed to grow as kids grow, adding more depth and relevant material at every level to help them stay curious about the world and to succeed at school and in life!

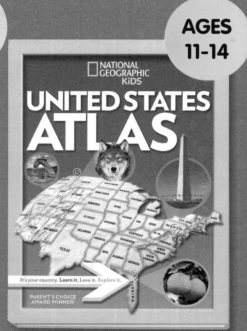

AGES 7-10

NATIONAL GEOGRAPHIC KiDS
BEGINNER'S
UNITED STATES
ATLAS

AGES 11-14

NATIONAL GEOGRAPHIC KiDS
UNITED STATES
ATLAS

It's your country. Learn it. Love it. Explore it.

PARENT'S CHOICE AWARD WINNER!

NATIONAL GEOGRAPHIC KiDS

AVAILABLE WHEREVER BOOKS ARE SOLD